Josip Lončar

The rosary - prayer of my spirit
The Joyful Mysteries

Josip Lončar
THE ROSARY
(JOYFUL MISTERIES)

PUBLISHED BY
Živo kamenje d.o.o., Međugorje

AUTHOR
Josip Lončar
fides@kristofori.hr

TRANSLATOR
Željka Juričić

CORRECTIONS
Paula Mužić B.A.Th.

THEOLOGICAL SUPERVISORS
Dr. fra Ivan Ivanda
Remigije Tomo Mlinarić, ofm

GRAPHIC DESIGN
Mislav Bošnjak

COVER
Mislav Bošnjak, Ružica Šilić

Printed in Bosnia and Herzegovina

PRINTED BY
FRAM ZIRAL, Mostar

COPYRIGHT
Živo kamenje d.o.o.

ISBN 978-9958-9115-3-8

CIP - Katalogizacija u publikaciji
Nacionalna i univerzitetska biblioteka
Bosne i Hercegovine, Sarajevo

272-534.35

LONČAR, Josip
     The rosary - prayer of my spirit : the joyful mysteries
/ Josip Lončar ; [translator Paula Wade Mužić]. - Čitluk :
Živo kamenje, 2007. - 184 str.

ISBN 978-9958-9115-3-8

COBISS.BH-ID 15879174

Scripture quotations are taken from the NRSV Catholic Edition / Oxford University Press.

Josip Lončar

The rosary
prayer of my spirit

THE JOYFUL MYSTERIES

Živo kamenje d.o.o., Međugorje

Foreword

The devotion of the rosary is a simple but powerful prayer. It has been practiced in Christianity since the sixth century. Through it, countless souls received the grace of conversion and salvation for their brothers and sisters. Jesus' Mother, in Lourdes and Fatima- just to mention two of the places she appeared in- spoke about the importance and the need for praying the rosary. She herself was holding the beads in her hand. Even so, it is a practice unfamiliar to many Christians. A great number heard of the rosary, but never actually prayed it themselves. There are probably even more who prayed it at one time in their lives, but gave it up. They hadn't realized its purpose nor had they discovered its inner beauty. For them, the repetition must have seemed pointless; just a mechanical verbal exercise. The truth is it is *completely* the opposite! The rosary is more a prayer of the heart than the mind. So how can we pray the rosary correctly and integrate it into our everyday life?

Josip Lončar, a recognized and well known charismatic, who, just a few years ago published *The Charism of Faith,* now offers another significant publication, *The rosary - prayer of my spirit.* I believe it will play a noteworthy role in the spiritual life of many of the faithful. In a unique way, the book opens our eyes to the depth, and the 'multi-layered nature' of this exceptional prayer, based on his personal prayer experience. His insights capture our attention in an interesting and impressive way. We feel like we are returning to something that we are already vaguely familiar with, but for some reason we had forgotten. We can compare it to returning to our lost homeland after years of being away. The book makes us ask ourselves can we really go on *without* the rosary. How can we neglect a prayer that has so much wealth? Of particular interest too in Lončar's book is his analysis of the individual mysteries of the rosary, demonstrating their connection with our own lives, pointing out what kind of liberation and healing we can expect to receive in each one of them. The testimonies and examples too, strike me as perfectly in harmony with the theme and somehow give weight and substance to the matter. I have mentioned just a few points of interest in the book because I do not wish to harm the humility of the writer. Each of you readers will see the value of the book for yourselves. I believe that it will whet your prayer appetite, which is one of the fundamental aims of the author. May Mary, the Queen of the Holy Rosary, bless both its writer and you the reader.

Dr. Ivan Ivanda. OFM

Introduction

The Catholic Church teaches that Mary is mediatrix of all graces, which means that in so far as we desire it, she can intercede for any grace that we ask of God. Of course there are Christians who maintain that Mary was just an ordinary woman, but this - dare I say it - is ignorance. But instead of condemning those who do not understand the plan of God with regard to her, let's do everything possible to put Mary in the right light! God loves all of his creatures and His wish is for all of us to be saved. In His enormous love towards us, He sent His only Son, who saved us through His passion, death and resurrection. He did all of this, in spite of our unworthiness. However, in order for this salvation to be effective in us- i.e. to be able to enjoy the fruits of that salvation- we have to accept it with our own free will and completely commit ourselves to God. God, given that He loves us, respects our free will - because without it - we are not complete people. For that reason, He waits for our willed acceptance of salvation (which He grants even though we do not deserve it): It includes life in God's will and co-operation in the salvation of all people.

Christ, as the head of the Mystical Body gave a complete and perfect 'offering' for our salvation, but we - who are limbs of Christ's Mystical Body (the

Church) - have to give our offering too. That offering can be made by us personally, by other members of the Church or by the whole of the faithful. Paul, the apostle, aware of this, when writing his epistle to the Colossians said:

> I am now rejoicing in my sufferings for your sake, and in my flesh I am completing what is lacking in Christ's afflictions for the sake of his body, that is, the church. I became its servant according to God's commission that was given to me for you, to make the word of God fully known, the mystery that has been hidden throughout the ages and generations but has now been revealed to his saints. To them God chose to make known how great among the Gentiles are his riches of the glory of this mystery, which is Christ in you, the hope of glory. It is he whom we proclaim, warning everyone and teaching everyone in all wisdom, so that we may present everyone mature in Christ. For this I toil and struggle with all the energy that he powerfully inspires within me. (Col 1.24-29)

In that *accepting of salvation for oneself* and *mediating it for others*, praying the rosary is extremely powerful. But because of free will, the possibility exists that an individual will *not* save himself and *not* go to heaven while thanks to the same free will, there is also a big possibility that an individual will use this gift and soar high in heaven! It is up to us to choose. Even though Jesus Christ is the only Mediator of Salvation between God and man, He cannot save anyone who doesn't seek and accept that same salvation (by personal prayer and belief, or by someone who is interceding on his/her behalf before God). This is so, because God is not biased and loves all men equally. In this book we are speaking about a particular type of mediation - intercession through the rosary.

The Father's offer of Salvation

I would like to begin by referring to a testimony, a true story that took place in the Republic of South Africa after apartheid finished. I heard it from Bishop Joe Greece during one of his Mass homilies. I'm not sure whether I'll manage to capture all the details in full, but I can remember the essence of the story.

After years of racial discrimination peace was finally proclaimed and trials were introduced to judge those who, during racial discrimination, carried out crimes. At one of those trials, there was an older lady sitting opposite a terrorist leader who had carried out war crimes against her family.

Let me tell you what had happened:

One day, the accused had come into this woman's home, and taken her husband away. The woman was left alone with her son. They were Catholics and they started praying for her husband, the boy's father. During that time they fervently prayed for their persecutors, especially for the leader of those terrorists, who was known to be exceptionally cruel. The family had nothing to do with politics and there were absolutely no grounds for this persecution. After six months they heard that the father had been killed after long-drawn-out tortures. They never received the corpse to bury him with dignity. The wife and son continued to pray for their persecutors. It was not long before the same man came to take the son. They killed him too without any proof that he had committed any offence. The woman forgave again, but she continued to pray for her persecutors. She did not despair because she knew that her husband and son were in God's hands. She knew that she didn't have to be afraid for them anymore. It was difficult to withstand the loneliness without her dear ones. But in her heart she never once cursed the people who were guilty. Instead she prayed to God that her persecutors wouldn't lose their eternal life because of all the wrongs they had commit against her family.

The people in that courtroom could discern the teachings of Jesus Christ when listening to her testimony. But still, nobody could have expected the turn of events that took place. The defendant's life really hung on a thread because the destiny of the man depended on two conditions. The first was that he would make sincere atonement. And the second was that the woman against whom he had committed the crimes had to forgive him.

Humanly speaking, he should have had very little chance of escaping the death penalty. At the end of her bearing witness, the lady was to say whether she would grant him his life or not. It was in her hands. Given that she had been talking about Jesus Christ and the resurrection of the dead, most expected her to forgive. In fact, she said that, as a Christian, she forgave him a long time ago, but if he wanted to live there was a third condition that he must fulfil.

Here we can stop for a moment to ask whether her decision to set conditions was Christian or not. As a Christian - after he had repented - should she have absolutely forgiven, or did she have the right to set some kind of condition?

Let's compare the situation with our own relationship with God. All of us are born with original sin and all of us are destined for spiritual death up until the moment of our baptism. All of us are born with the fault of our predecessors. Adam and Eve, by their sin rejected God's love and in that way, they 'killed' God inside them. Therefore they lost the right to eternal life. What was most terrible in their sin was their mistrust of God's fairness; they discarded God. How many Christians today think that God is unfair and mistrust him! How many Christians today will still eagerly eat from the forbidden tree? And God is killed once again! Many Christians believe that the Jews with the help of the Romans killed Jesus on the cross, but Jesus didn't die as a consequence of physical abuse. His heart stopped beating due to the immense sorrow when he 'saw' (there is no tense in English that expresses an ability to see down through the ages) that the majority of mankind would reject Him and show Him that distrust. So those that caused His death were not only His contemporaries. Jesus from the cross 'saw' all of us who would meet Him down through the centuries, and then reject Him as God and as Love. I must admit that I was one of them, given that, for years I didn't want to accept Him as my Lord. He could see the millions of Christians who didn't want God as their Father, who didn't want to listen to his Word and live by His Spirit which would have been best for them. He saw that people would love the world for its pleasures and hold to the outer forms of worship, but at the same time deny its power. They wouldn't care for God. They wouldn't need the God, Jesus (See 2 Tim 3: 1-5).

Most Christians today don't want God as their Father! If we honestly think about Jesus' longing for our love (as seen on the cross), or on the Father's longing for us, (which is why he sacrificed his only Son), can any of us be absolutely sure that we didn't ever, in our lifetime, participate in the killing of God's Son on the cross? Mark the Evangelist, writes that Pilate was surprised that Jesus died so fast. The soldiers were also surprised by Jesus' fast death. Their experience in crucifying people led them to expect that His agony would last a lot longer. This leads us to conclude that it couldn't have just been the physical wounding that caused His death, but also the spiritual wounding.

When we consider that Adam with his sin renounced God, and in that way lost the possibility for God to grant him eternal life, how can we consider that the disobeying His commandments or His Word in general is any less dangerous? We bring ourselves into a situation of being sentenced to death. God mercifully forgives us after we sincerely repent, but if we *really* want to live, that's not enough. God also sets conditions for our life even though He forgives us! There is the possibility that all our sins will be forgiven but we still cannot inherit eternal life.

The lady in the court-room knew God and knew about that condition. She knew what God expected of everyone who wished to repent of having 'killed God' on the cross. She knew what the prerequisites were - if the repentance was sincere - in order for him to be able to live again.

The words she addressed to the murderer of her son and husband were, "If you wish to live, and I personally want you to live, you have to accept me as your mother. First, you must hug me. Then you will come with me to my house and live with me up till my last days, as an adopted son. I am old and needy not just of physical help, but I am also in need of love which gives me spiritual strength. I wish you to replace my son and do all the things he would now be doing for me if he were still alive. That's what I wish for."

The man to whom the words were addressed, on hearing them fainted. Here I will finish my account of this testimony. Instead of wondering whether the man accepted the lady's offer to be her adopted son, let's ask whether we accepted the offer to be adopted sons to the Father, in place of His Son who was crucified.

In short, if we honestly wish to live after we have sinned, we have to take up where Jesus left off.... We have to love our Father the way He loved Him. Above all we have to continue the work that Jesus started. His job was to save souls. We cannot do that literally, because souls are saved only by Jesus' sacrifice of blood, but someone has to *bring* that soul before Jesus.

The necessity of prayer

The name of our job is evangelizer! Evangelization is a word which covers everything that a person can do by God's strength and his own spiritual and physical effort to bring people to Jesus Christ, the only one who can save them. Primarily, this means prayer which is why I am writing this book. Everything begins and ends with prayer. If we acquire knowledge about our faith and begin to practice what the Church teaches us but we don't learn how to pray, our life will be without the fruits which we, as children of God, ought to present. Our devotion will have no strength and it will turn into a cult, that lacks the power to change anyone, least of all ourselves.

Having held many seminars teaching people about God, and prayed for their needs, I realized that I won't do anything if I don't teach them how to pray. If we learn how to pray- prayer will raise evangelizers who will carry the Word to places where people still haven't heard it or where they haven't been taught it in the proper way. Those evangelizers won't achieve anything if they themselves don't know how to pray and unless other Christians support them with their prayers.

The rosary is one of the most extraordinary prayers which God gave to us and for that reason I decided to write about it.

A testimony

"I am sixteen years of age and I would like to testify to the experience I had about our living God. I grew up in a Catholic family, even though it seemed to me we were more of a Catholic family 'on paper' then in practice. My grandmother taught me how to pray, but up till my schooling I can not remember whether my parents ever took me to Mass. In first grade elementary school I was barely able to talk my parents into allowing me to attend catechism at school. Then I began to go to Mass. Unfortunately, while other children were coming with their families I was coming on my own. Nevertheless I never felt left out. In Church I always felt I was protected, given security and loved. After my first Holy Communion my mother began to go to Mass with me because I became an altar boy for about ten years. Today when my mother finds it difficult because we are on our own, she often thanks me for taking her to church, because that was when she started to believe

I had a difficult childhood because my parents separated about five years ago. Through that whole period the only hope and consolation I had was my Lord. Even though I was only eleven years old and I didn't understand a lot of things, there was one thing I was sure of; that God loved me! His love encouraged me to help my mother carry on, persevering despite the fact that she felt that she could never get back up after such a heavy fall.

But when things got back to normal, I have to admit that my faith gradually became a routine thing. I can still remember the holidays between seventh and eighth grade when for almost two months I didn't even go to Mass. My faith turned into a habit and I preferred to spend my free time with my friends instead of with God. I still went to Mass, but it wasn't because I truly wished to be with God, but more out of habit and fulfilling Church obligations- right up to my Confirmation May 4, 2003. I returned to God with my whole heart and firmly decided to follow Him. It was difficult because all my friends were laughing at me. For them, faith and the Church were the last things on their minds. For them outings, habitual drinking, and other pleasures were more important. In their world I was abnormal. Nevertheless I endured and went on to High school. There I found new friends who did not make fun of me because of my faith. In reality, I wasn't alone anymore because in my grade there were girls I met at the spiritual renewals held in the convent with the nuns.

One Christmas around Christmas 2003 I had an incredible experience of the living Jesus in the Eucharist. After I received Holy Communion, I felt great warmth, an amazing love- as if I was standing in a fire. I decided then, that I would be an even better person and give my life to God.

Two months later, in February of 2004 a friend invited me to attend a charismatic meeting with him. I didn't know what it was, but as soon as he explained that it's just a meeting to praise our Lord, I accepted straight away. We went and it was wonderful: Mass, praising, togetherness...it made me feel really special. The theme of the encounter was *the rosary - prayer of my spirit*. After the talk, Josip began praying the sorrowful mysteries. He asked us to close our eyes, to enter our heart, to meet with God in our heart and to stay in peace listening to the rosary, to allow each word to enter our heart. Once again I felt the same fire I felt two months previous when I received Holy Communion, but now it was even stronger. During the prayer Josip spoke about the individual mysteries and I started receiving live pictures of the tortures which Jesus underwent for us. I felt His living presence beside me and I felt His hand resting on my head. The whole time, tears were flowing and flowing, but I didn't notice them. When the prayer finished, I opened my eyes and realized that I was wet: my whole face, my hair, everything....

And to my disbelief after a short time I was completely dry. I didn't understand what happened, but I was very happy. During the rosary my life changed from its roots upwards. It was as if God fulfilled my prayer for a complete deliverance!

When I went to Mass the next day, I realized, each time I looked at a crucifix or started praying the rosary, pictures of Jesus' tortures would come in front of my eyes, whether I wanted it or not.

Two weeks after the Charismatic Seminar, I was watching the film *The Passion,* at home with friends. When the scene appeared where he was whipped, after the first whip lash, I felt a pain which I had never felt before. I started to shake and began to cry. My friend who was sitting beside me put my head on her lap so that I would not watch and covered my ears so that I would not hear what was happening in the film. Even though I wasn't watching those scenes, I could see it all in my head. I stopped watching the film and I needed time to calm down and be myself again. Tears were just flowing and I couldn't stop them. But I still wanted to watch the film to the end. I shook and trembled every time that Jesus was struck or insulted. And the same happened when I watched the crucifixion. At the moment that He died on the cross, I felt exhausted, tired. I stopped crying, sighed and drifted into sleep. I opened my eyes again and it was the scene of the Resurrection. My friends who were sitting beside me told me because I wasn't really conscious. I was there, on Golgotha! I saw how they were taking Jesus down from the cross and placing Him in the tomb. I was there! I died and together with Him arose! From that day onwards, precisely at 3p.m. I shook and cried as the pictures of Our Lords Passion were renewed before my eyes spontaneously. It would last for about 5 minutes, after which I would fall asleep (deep enough so that I couldn't be wakened) and then when I would come around everything would be normal again- except for one thing: my love towards our Lord would be even greater!

I was sent to a psychiatrist to examine me and my brain was x-rayed because all this was now happening to me at school in front of everybody. My test results were normal and the doctors confirmed that I was completely healthy, physically and mentally.

The spiritual experience of the tortures still happens to me, but not every day, mainly on the first Fridays of every month and more often during the season of Lent. It's at its' worst on Holy Thursday night. I had to pass a lot of trials that night. I couldn't sleep all night long. It was as if someone put a heavy rock on my heart which was pulling me down. I felt an anxiety which prevented me from sleeping, I cried and cried.

I still cannot fully comprehend all of this but I do know: everything that I feel and everything that I will continue to endure is for the greater honour and glory of our Lord, and that's why it brings me a deep joy. What I endure is just a trifle compared to what He endured for our sins. And He is always with me. He says to me, "Do not be afraid, I am with you. You are not on your own in this world. Believe me."

I put my life in His hands and He takes care of me. I can feel how much He loves me! The Lord is always with me and there is nothing I shall want. And me? I am just a tool in His hands. I can only pray that He gives me the strength to carry in the face of obstacles, that He gives me humility and patience, that He allows me to share my experiences with others so that they can accept Him as their Saviour and Redeemer, so that the love that is burning in me may be passed on to others who are in need of His love and consolation. That is all I can offer, my whole self!"

Why do I call it
– *my grandmother's rosary?*

The rosary of the Blessed Virgin Mary must be one of the most loved prayers in the Catholic Church today. It can be prayed in a number of ways, all of which have their own value. Having travelled around the shrines of Europe, I am even more convinced of that now. It's not necessary though to travel the whole of Europe to see this. It is enough just to go to one particular place where the whole world gathers. There are many shrines dedicated to the Blessed Virgin Mary. In my country, Croatia, there are several, but it is definitely a special experience to go to Medjugorje if you are interested in the rosary. There, you can see people of all different skin colour from all over the world holding the rosary in their hands and praying.

Personally, my experience with the rosary began with my Grandmother who has since passed away. My family prayed regularly, especially before and after meals. They prayed the Angelus too, three times a day. But I cannot ever remember that we prayed the rosary together as a family. I know that my parents prayed it but they didn't expect us kids to pray it along with them.

My grandmother was widowed and so for a long time she lived alone in her house. Everyone in the village knew that she was religious. Visiting her occasionally, I presumed that all she ever did all day was pray. The rest of the time she spent cooking something quickly (if she wasn't fasting). For her, the television didn't exist. We all knew that she was a holy and special woman. The blessings on our family were so evident that many of us used to ask ourselves how come we were so lucky. After her death, it was clear where it had come from. Those of us who continued the prayer tradition in the family continued to thrive, while those that did not spend time in prayer slowly but surely sank-I won't say cursed- but the blessings slowly dwindled. One thing was sure: After her death a lot of things changed.

I will never forget one particular day when I visited my grandmother. I was only ten. My grandmother stood me in front of her and said with great seriousness: "If you wish to have luck in your life, you have to pray to Our Lady to take care and guide you and the Holy Spirit to enlighten your mind!" It was the first time in my life that I knew- I don't know how I knew- that the words didn't come from my grandmother or any mortal being. She was just a means; it was God who spoke through her. Those words cut deeply into my memory and have followed me for thirty years now.

Now I can see that my grandmother did the most useful job possible in her old age. If only other grandfathers and grandmothers knew what they are failing to do when they have neither the time nor the desire to represent their descendants in prayer, or at least communicate their prayer experience to their grandchildren. Is today's generation not feeling the reverberations of that lack of love?

Prayer for my grandmother - especially the prayer of the rosary - was a joy. Once again- I don't know how I know- but I know she prayed it in exactly the way that I pray it now and I have to show it to others. My intention is that the prayer of the rosary becomes, not just a commitment, but that primarily it becomes a joy, secondly a powerful weapon in the battle against evil, and finally a splendid way of obtaining blessings!

In no way do I wish to belittle any other way of praying the rosary, but rather to add one more pearl to that already priceless treasure.

How can the rosary be - prayer in the spirit?

Everything began after my wife and I participated in a joint *Renewal in the spirit* seminar. It happened to both of us on practically the same day. Shortly afterwards many charisms began to manifest themselves in both of us. It took place at one of the first seminars for the outpouring of the Holy Spirit in our area. There were three priests and about ten lay persons present. At that seminar, which started on a Thursday and finished on the following Sunday, the Holy Spirit was strongly present and dramatic 'new births' took place. The climax was on the Saturday evening, during a prayer for the outpouring of the gifts: The Holy Spirit released itself so overwhelmingly that most of us were frightened. It was a really powerful outpouring on that tiny community. Shortly after that we spoke in different languages, some received the gift of tongues, some the gift of healing, some the gift of miracles, others the gift of prophecy, utterance of knowledge...etc.

One of the more significant gifts which my wife Mirjana received -for the service of the community - was the gift of knowledge which manifested itself through visions. She received them practically every time she prayed. During prayer, visions would present themselves, which she didn't know how to explain. I received the gift (spiritual ability) to know exactly what each vision meant. On that basis alone, you can see how that meant that our prayer time was by no means boring. The visions were systematically clarified during prayer together, we always knew their meaning.

There was one exception. When she prayed the rosary, often in a very vivid vision, the image of an unknown woman would present itself. That would often happen when she prayed in Church. The profile of the woman was very clear, but we didn't know who it was. I didn't know what that vision meant but we assumed we had to pray for that person or maybe God wanted to tell us something special through her. After a few months we actually met that person. She was a Catholic charismatic evangelizer who played a significant role in our lives. Amongst other things, before she met us, she gave a prophecy which was linked to the evangelization work intended for our community. When we finally met her, she approached me and spoke prophetically. Although it was completely unacceptable at that time, later it completely changed the course of my life. When she finished with me, telling me that I would lead a work of evangelization, she said that the Holy Spirit was telling her that there is another person who is chosen to help me in that work. We were in a large parking area and my wife at that time was about 50 meters away from us. Let me just state that the lady knew absolutely nothing about me or my wife (neither had she heard anything about us from anyone), so she couldn't have known that we were a married couple.

However, at that moment, she noticed Mirjana. She turned towards her and spoke a prophecy for her too. Mirjana didn't understand anything because the prophecy was in English. But what surprised Mirjana was that she recognized the woman as the one in her visions while praying the rosary!

Since then so many things have happened. For example, on the same day that Mirjana and I prayed for a twelve year old girl, who was deaf and mute from birth, after the prayers, she received her hearing and started to speak her first words. In the time following the prayer, she completely recovered. There is one thing I am sure of: what ever plans God has for us, it will be through our Lady. Didn't He show us that clearly?

Later, while praying the rosary, various people were coming in front of us in spirit, mostly in visions. I came to understand that this was something that wasn't coming from me, but 'someone' is *bringing* them into my spirit, although I wasn't sure of what exactly was happening. Even though the visions came during the time of my praying the rosary, they didn't disturb my concentration of prayer, i.e. this manifestation did not take away from the quality of my prayer. Mirjana had similar experiences. We came to realize that each vision came with its own prayer intention. We could see that it was possible to pray with the mind and the spirit at the same time.

I enquired around to see if there any others having similar experiences. A lady from our community told us of her first experience. One day while praying the rosary, she was able to see very clearly a face of a lady in one of her visions. She did not know her. She did not know how to explain it, but what was most interesting about the vision was that it didn't interrupt her prayer, nor did it disturb her. A few times the vision reoccurred and always on a particular mystery. She did not talk about it to anyone. After a certain period of time she went to hospital for a check up and seeing there was a crowd in the waiting room, she sat on a bench, closed her eyes and started praying the rosary with her eyes shut. Then one of the women beside her started to tell the woman beside her of her difficulties and the story stopped her from praying the rosary further. She started listening to the problems with interest. In short the lady had had a series of problems over a given period of time but they mysteriously started to resolve themselves. The lady who had been praying opened her eyes and guess who she saw? Precisely! the woman who would come into her spirit during prayer.

I remember the first time that my wife and I had the experience of being - shut out from time as we know it - during prayer. We prayed for about six hours, but we felt as if we prayed for a few minutes we decided that, in gratitude, we would each pray something special. Mirjana chose to pray the rosary in gratitude but I insisted on praying in tongues even though she wanted both of us to pray the rosary. Both of us started to pray our own prayers out loud. After a few moments she started to laugh out loud and stopped - she said that actually I had been praying the rosary too!

For those who do not know I would like to explain that praying in tongues is one of the charisms which the Holy Spirit gives us, which manifests itself as if we were speaking an unknown language. No one can understand the person who is praying apart from God and the person to whom God would give the gift of understanding of those tongues. When we pray in tongues, my spirit prays and my mind is not bound to the prayer. The prayer takes place in the Holy Spirit and we can be sure that what we are praying for is definitely God's wish for us (See 1. Cor 14). According to the ICCRS (the International Catholic Charismatic Renewal Services, office in the Vatican, Piazza della Cancelleria), about ninety million people have the gift of tongues today. Mirjana had the gift of interpretation of tongues, so that she was able to understand that I was actually praying the rosary in tongues. For me that was an important gesture from God to show me that all my charismatic experience is closely linked with Mary, just as the Holy Spirit is inexorably linked with her.

The charismatic community that I was leading at that time were mostly people who were deeply devoted to Our Lady. With the exception of one married couple for whom praying the rosary was basically "jibberish" They tried to convince us that it was wrong to pray to saints and to Mary, using biblical arguments. The only thing that they really convinced us was that they didn't belong in our group. But I found myself asking how can it be that people who really love God and serve Him in an effective way don't know the real truth about His role as our Saviour and the role of His Mother Mary in Him.

The follow up

We continued praying in the same manner and various people, some unknown to us, came into our prayer in the spirit in various ways. Here I must state that this is a gift which comes from God. Not everyone can have this prayer ability and this goes for any of the other gifts. Some of us had actual visions, while others 'recognized' intentions which they received in the spirit during prayer. Some experienced something like thoughts whereby they could hear the names of people who would come and their intentions; others had visions, while others would hear inner voices in a spiritual way. There were many other ways when praying the rosary that we recognized people or situations which would come through intentions, but the one thing that was common to all of us was that the 'information' would not disrupt our prayer. When the intention comes in spirit, it is up to us to simply continue praying with the mind, completely focused on what we are praying. There isn't a conscious effort not to think about the things we see and hear. The person that comes to us in spirit, (known or unknown, living or dead, one or more simultaneously) stay a shorter or a longer period of time in our spirit in front of us until they disappear. After that, the next one comes etc. We don't participate with our thoughts, or emotions in the actual intention, but we take the person through Mary and offer them to God in the Spirit. At the same time, our spirit is full of expectations, and full of gratitude for that person.

After a certain period of time we were able to see that certain people came practically every time we prayed a particular mystery. This was allowed so that we could sometimes see the results of our prayers. There were even a few particular cases when someone would be in danger of death (in a car accident for example), from which they would emerge completely untouched to the astonishment of the onlookers. Later it would be established that on the same day that person came into our intentions while praying the rosary.

I realized that every mystery is a fountain of certain sorts of blessings and that a deep understanding of the mysteries paved the way to this sort of prayer. I began to teach people this sort of rosary, although for a long time, I didn't have a name for it. Now I will refer to it as, *"The rosary - prayer of my spirit"* (in the original version of the book written in Croatian, the title is "Bakina Krunica"-meaning-my grandmothers rosary not just in memory of her, but also so that the way she prayed can be of example to others.) This world would change in a lot of ways for the better if more grandmothers and grandfathers desired to be children of the Father, and undertake Jesus' mission to pray.

Whenever I speak about this kind of prayer I encounter enthusiasm in the faithful. Young people who are usually stubborn about going to church, not to mention serious belief and prayer, start to pray the rosary. Even some who never thought they would pray. Most of them immediately believe in the strength of that sort of rosary.

The Charism of faith in
'The rosary - prayer of my spirit'

After the Creed and the initial Our Father, the first Hail Mary that we pray is addressed to Jesus in petition to multiply our faith. Faith is one of the most important elements in every prayer and this is also true of the rosary. In *Charism of Faith,* my first book, I completely dedicated it to understanding faith, so here I will only touch upon it.

Searching through Sacred Scripture, I found just one place that gives a definition of *the charism of faith.* It was in St. Paul's epistle to the Hebrews. I must admit that when I came across the content of the definition, it really surprised me. Aspects that had puzzled me up until then, started to fit into place. Let's take a look at what the greatest 'Apostle of Faith' said about faith:

> (Heb 11.1-3)
> *Now faith is the assurance of things hoped for, the conviction of things not seen.*
>
> *Indeed by faith our ancestors received approval. By faith we understand that the worlds were prepared by the word of God, so that what is seen was made from things that are not visible.*

35

Let's now analyse that first sentence, section by section.

Now faith is the assurance of things hoped for...
the conviction of things unseen.

If we are to pray with faith, we have to satisfy the conditions in the definition of faith. The first condition is the assurance of things hoped for, the knowledge that what we are praying for belongs to us as part of the inheritance won for us by the Son. This was won by His death on the cross; in other words, the first condition is that our request be in accordance with Jesus' will. Let's take a little look at John's Gospel:

(Jn 14: 14)
If in my name you ask me for anything, I will do it

(Jn 15.16)
... so that the Father will give you whatever you ask him in my name. [7]

(Jn 16.23-24)
Truly, truly I say to you if you ask anything of the Father, he will give it to you in my name. Hitherto you have asked nothing in my name; ask and you will receive, that your joy may be complete.

When we receive the assurance in our hearts that what we are praying for is in accordance with Jesus' will then we have a warrant to ask the Father in His name. In this way the granting of prayer becomes part of the 'mission' undertaken in His name, in other words, through the right which accompanies the assurance. The realization of this prayer therefore, is something that we, with spiritual authorization in the spiritual world, 'carry out', in His name, things which will be made in the realms in which *we* live.

In this kind of prayer, we are God's servants, and we merely carry out His will. We comprehend that prayer is often like Jacob's *wrestling* with God. We have to find the assurance so that we can know that we are Jesus' successors and we have to prove that what we are looking for is part of that inheritance - that is - that what we are looking for is part of Jesus Will for us. First we have to prove to *ourselves* since God and the devil already know this. This assurance gives us the ability to 'step' in front of God with confidence and receive the response to our request!

Whatever we receive from God is the result of God's love towards us. Jesus came so that the sheep will have life and an abundance of it. In our inheritance, He left us the fullness of blessings and there is not a prayer forwarded to God in love with faith which has not already been fulfilled in Christ. Reading and reflecting on the Sacred Scriptures we become acquainted with our inheritance and the magnitude of God's mercy. We receive confidence in His Word and His love and in that way we find the assurance needed for receiving faith and the answer to our prayers.

Satan is the one who came to steal, destroy and kill. He is our constant accuser. What does he steal from us? He steals the inheritance which is ours through the testament. He is a liar from the beginning. What does he lie about? He lies to us telling us that we do not have the right to our inheritance. He tries to pervert the truth about the validity of the last will. (See Gal 4.1-7, and Rom 8.12-17) In our hearts we must possess the assurance that what we are asking for is truly what belongs to us as God's children, as inheritors of Christ. Satan is accusing us of not being worthy to accept that inheritance. If we haven't got that assurance in our hearts, it will be difficult to receive faith of the heart. We cannot then hope to have our prayers answered because God's word tells us that those who doubt are similar to sea waves and double-minded and unstable in every way. For that reason they cannot expect to receive anything from God. (See Jam 1.6-8)

But when we have that assurance, we have arrived at the first part of faith. The second consists of conviction. Conviction of what? The second part of the first sentence defining faith is:

Now faith is..., the conviction of things not seen.

Distinct faith is needed for each prayer respectively. For every petition we have to have a respective assurance and a respective conviction. Do we not pray at the beginning of every rosary for Jesus to multiply our faith? Therefore the assurance is something we are looking for, and conviction is something we receive as an endorsement of our prayer being granted when we come before God with firm assurance in our hearts.

Let's take a better look and we will see that St. Paul talks about some sort of things (see Heb 11.1) that we cannot see, but that nevertheless exist because God has prepared them in advance for us. For us to comprehend what those things are, we will take another look at another two places in Sacred Scripture.

(Mk 11.24)
So I tell you, whatever you ask for in prayer, believe that you have received it, and it will be yours.

(1 Jn 5.14-15)
And this is the boldness we have in him, that if we ask anything according to his will he hears us. And if we know that he hears us in whatever we ask, we know that we have obtained the requests made of him.

What Paul the Apostle points out in the definition of faith is confirmed by the evangelist John and Mark. All three say that the things which we are praying for exist already before we started to pray for them. Therefore, when we pray, we pray to God to give us something that already exists.

Reading and reflecting on God's written Word, we discover what those things already exist. By prayer in the Holy Spirit, they are brought into our spirit so that we can 'see' them. Then that 'seeing' becomes the conviction of our faith. We mentioned before that Paul, the Apostle says that the faithful interact in the area of faith, (i.e. with spiritual eyes) and not in the area of seeing (with physical eyes)

When we bring our sickness, or any other suffering before God, then in faith, we will receive what God thinks is best for us. What God chooses is the best possible gift for us - whether it is healing or acceptance of suffering as a willing sacrifice. Both bring the presence of God and an element of joy to those who receive the gift. If we don't receive joy or peace from the influence of God in our situation, it means that we still did not receive the second part of our faith, that is, the conviction that God heard and accepted our prayer. When we have the conviction that God has accepted our prayers, then we have 'complete faith' by which God can at the right time and the right place produce what we prayed for with faith. Sometimes it happens immediately during prayer, but sometimes a lot of time has to pass. However, we can be assured that it will be 'made' (see Heb 11.3) if we prayed with faith. It is not necessary to pray further for that purpose; we just have to praise God and glorify Him sincerely. Glorifying and praising 'disables' Satan from stealing what belongs to us - what we have received through praying with faith. So we know then that all our prayer forwarded to God we have to have a special, or perhaps it would be better to say, its own portion of faith.

The Word of God tells us that faith comes from preaching (see Rom 10.17). It is true that our confidence really increases when preaching is designed in such a way that we can receive that assurance which is needed for the actualization of our prayers, or, when a homily demonstrates the love of God towards us and highlights the obstacles which keep us from God. They also inspire us when they speak of God's will for us, which is just love and nothing else or when it is a personal testimony of prayer in faith. Trust paves the way to faith. What is most important in a homily is that the spoken word is truly inspired by the Holy Spirit for the particular time and place where the listeners find themselves. The preacher has to preach in such a way that those listening can feel what the two disciples felt when walking with Jesus towards Emmaus. They said,

(Lk 24.32).
Were not our hearts burning within us while he spoke to us on the way and opened the scriptures to us?

Most of today's homilies are born from our sense of *reason*, which unfortunately cannot see the spiritual reality. The homilies can be interesting and illuminating, but they do not have that same strength as those inspired by the Holy Spirit. The word of God wants to bring us that faith by which we can ask favours of God. The right relationship towards God then, and towards what we are praying for, needs to be taught to us in homilies.

I would like to stress once again that faith comes from preaching when that preaching is the Word of Christ. However, faith also 'comes' from listening to the testimonies of those, who have encountered the mercy of God or who were witnesses to it. This is the reason why, to those who had not yet heard testimonies about the things he had done elsewhere, Jesus first preached and then performed miracles. There, faith was granted to them as a consequence of the word of God, heard through preaching.

The best and the simplest homilies are those that come alive when we ourselves begin to look up the Word of God by reading the Bible, when we have confidence that the author, that is, the Holy Spirit, explains the way he wants to when we read with confidence, He will speak His living Word. Perhaps it would be better to say *He will open the eyes of our heart to 'see' what is actually written.* Jesus told us that the written word is hidden from the intellect and the mind and only infants can have real revelations about it. What He means is those that do not see themselves as wise and intelligent (see Lk 10.21). In truth, our minds are really limited so we can all be 'little' in accepting the Word of God as it is written, without devising our own 'intelligent explanation', which really only serves to justify our own lack of faith. That is why we're all called to feed ourselves with the Word of God. Pope John Paul II said that we have too many teachers, and not enough witnesses, that is, too much theory and not enough practice.

Sacred Scripture tells us that an heir must be of age in order to take his inheritance in full (see Gal 4.1-2). Did we not come of age with the Sacrament of Confirmation?

The person who prays with faith possesses the solution to many problems. The faithful, as sons of God, are the owners of unbelievable wealth, through which they can show love to many people around them. Maybe we take this "unfaithfully". But let's take a look at how Peter and John showed love towards a man who was lame from birth! The lame man asked for grace, but Peter only gave him what he had. Let's take a look:

(Acts 3.6)
But Peter said: "I have no silver or gold, but **what I do have** *I give you; in the name of Jesus Christ of Nazareth, stand up and walk."*

The lame man walked. Peter claimed that what he did have was the health that belonged to the lame man. In a certain way, we as children of God, possess all inheritance jointly which we can distribute on one condition, that is, the condition of our faith.

Paul the Apostle says that some believe that we Christians are poor, but in fact we are the ones that possess everything (See 2 Cor 6.10). Everything is at our disposal, even though we don't take everything. Can anyone say that God does not want to give us something that is good for us? The truth is that either we do not know whether it is good or not or we do not take it. One or the other!

That means that every heir or 'son in faith' has access to the treasures of any power or authority by which he can show love and mercy to those around him (see Eph 1.15-21).

When praying the rosary, we come before Mary and before God with conviction in our heart that the blessings we seek are at our disposal. We do this so that by God's intervention, we can bring blessings into our lives and the lives of others whom Mary presents before the throne of God in the rosary. We enter this prayer with clear knowledge that God is interested in answering our prayers, because His name is Love.

Studying and meditating on the individual mysteries, we get to know this *assurance*. The Holy Spirit can then lead us into the wealth of God's mercy, shown through individual mysteries of Jesus' life. Insight about these mysteries will continue to deepen throughout our whole lives. During prayer time, our spirit is open to the help of the Holy Spirit. He can bring various people who are in need into our spirit. The number and frequency of intentions will depend on our openness of spirit and the magnitude of God's gift.

Here we notice a difference from the usual charismatic prayers of faith. When we pray the '*The rosary*

- prayer of my spirit', we have a certainty, an assurance in our hearts regarding individual needs through reflecting on the mysteries.

For example, the first sorrowful mystery, we know that it is suited to praying for anyone under the influence of various types of fear, stress, depression, psychological sicknesses, those who experience no hope, but also anyone under demonic oppression or possession such as magic, sorcery and other types of curses. Praying with the mind, we focus on the actual words we utter. With our hearts we focus on Our Blessed Mother and God, but simultaneously in our spirit, we carry the favour that we seek in prayer. At the same time the Holy Spirit inspires us with intentions, people and situations (we can seek so much in prayer, we don't need to limit ourselves to people) which through the individual mysteries can be blessed. In our spirit, we're immersed in God in whom the whole prayer takes place. When we truly have that gift, we are capable of recognizing the intentions which come to us in the spirit through prayer. In this state, we don't need to tie ourselves to the individual intentions with mind and heart; we let the Holy Spirit decide the duration of the individual revelation and its intensity. This shouldn't distract our mind and heart at all. It can even happen that we can stay in the presence of God for hours and don't even realize that so much time has passed by, but this type of prayer usually has its own rhythm. It is my belief that this type of prayer is impossible without the help of the Holy Spirit.

It is important that the intentions that come to us during that prayer are not the fruits of our own desires, either consciously, or as in contemplation unconsciously. If the Holy Spirit is the one that brings someone or something into our prayers, that automatically means that the prayer is carried out in His will, and that He decided to bless that person in a specific way. The blessing has something to do with the mystery of the rosary, during which the intercession for that person took place. Just the appearance of that person in our spirit is exactly the second half of our faith, the conviction that the prayer has been heard and granted. We have been shown how that functions so many times. Jesus himself tells us that the Father is drawing us to himself! And very often this happens through Mary's intercession.

Prayer as an encounter - with expectations

There are encounters which leave us full of expectations and others from which we don't really expect anything. We can bump into somebody by sheer coincidence. Sometimes we hope we do bump into someone or it can happen that we really hope we don't bump into them. If we have planned a meeting, generally we have some sort of expectation from it, big or small. Maybe we should ask ourselves what we are expecting from the meeting. If it's a chance meeting, it can still happen that that we have unconscious expectations - although it doesn't have to be that way. How much we expect depends on the person we are meeting and our needs at the time, spiritual or material. It also depends on our state of mind and the disposition of the person or persons we will meet.

An encounter from which we are expecting something (either to receive, to give or to share) differs from the meetings that are routine or coincidental.

Prayer is an encounter; a personal encounter with my own God (the One that I know). If I wish to encounter Mary or someone else from heaven, it is a meeting that takes place together with God. In other words, in prayer we cannot meet anyone unless the Holy Spirit makes it possible. So we really need to be aware that when we 'meet' or 'find ourselves' with Mary, for example, we do so in communion with God. We even say *...the lord is with thee,* aware of the fact that our encounter with Our Lady is happening in God.

Every prayer uttered should be a comprehensive encounter with God at the level of the spirit, the soul and the body. In this it is both similar to and very different from our encounters here on earth. One of the things it has in common is that element of *expecting* or *not expecting.* Our expectation is linked with our *love of God.*

Through meditation, we come to know God as a loving Father, but at the same time as the almighty Creator, the only Saviour and Redeemer. This awakens within us a spiritual expectation of His love towards us and towards the whole of creation. At the same time our spirit expects to be able to respond to His love at every encounter.

When I looked back on my experience of prayer, I came to an interesting conclusion which changed my way of prayer from its roots up. I would like all my prayer experiences to be full of spiritual expectation, united in love with Him. This is possible because I know that God wants it too. The world is in need of God's mercy like never before. Millions of people have still not heard the messages of the Gospel, millions live in mortal sin, millions suffer and there is no meaning or purpose to their suffering. The world is full of wars, earthquakes and catastrophes, hunger, oppression and violence. Many are lonely, bitter, misunderstood and live with the impression of being abandoned. Jesus died for every one of them, not just for me. But His mercy comes only to those who have been interceded for.

God is not biased and can act only when asked to through prayer. He is saddened because there are not enough mediators, who by their prayers would obtain His mercy for those in need. (Is 59.16)

God in all our encounters with Him wants us to 'open' our hearts in expectation of his graces so that they would flow through us to those in need and to ourselves too. The enormity of his mercy is matched only by how much this world needs His mercy. If God could find enough people who have adequate expectations, He would be able to change the whole world with His mercy.

Unfortunately, too often our expectations are low. God is calling us to love - to love one another the way He loves us. If we analyse our prayers and ask ourselves, in what way and with how much expectation we pray, then we will be able to see how open our heart is to His mercy and the needs of our fellow man. How will we receive faith if we do not ask with the expectation to receive it?!

We often pray to Jesus to make our heart like His heart. What would happen if every day for a month, we prayed, *Jesus, meek and lowly of heart, make my heart like unto thine own*? Quite a lot of things would be overturned inside us! What would happen then if for one hour every day we were to intensively consider those who are mostly in need of God's mercy in order to be saved? They are people who need soothing and comforting in suffering, or who simply need to learn how to really love. In the act of considering, we give the Holy Spirit the possibility to stimulate our spirit and change it. Our spirit is greatly influenced by the considerations taking place in the mind (See Eph 4.23).

It is extremely important to acknowledge our weaknesses and imperfections. If we are aware of them and realize that despite our faults we are still accepted, then it won't be difficult for us to see that God loves us and all other sinners equally. Not a single one of us converted by our own merits, but rather it was a grace interceded for us by someone else. Most of us converted unexpectedly. However, someone else planned it instead of us: Someone interceded for us before God. Someone's sincere longing in a prayer of faith, was enough for God's grace to surprisingly touch us and change our heart. Whoever has had an experience of that knows that for God nothing is impossible.

In every prayer of petition, we should anticipate a lot from the encounter with Him. We have to realize that the world is in need of His mercy and that our imperfections shouldn't limit His love. God loves me despite the fact that I am weak. My weakness doesn't prevent Him from approaching me. Why should I then prevent Him from working through me? If I wish, then I expect, if I expect then I believe. Let's take a look at the book *Story of a soul*, by St Teresa of the child Jesus.

"As a bright child, I realized that I wanted to be everything, to have all careers and to have wealth which could have easily made me unjust, because I would use it to win friends .....Then I remembered Elisha's prayer to his father Elijah, when he dared to ask for a double portion of his father's spirit (see 2 Kings 2.9). I prayed in the company of the angels and saints and told them: "I am the unworthiest of creatures, I know my misery and weakness but I know how much a noble and generous heart does good. So I beg you to take me as your child, the only thing that you shall receive will be the glory of the things I do with your help. Deign to answer my prayer, I know it is audacious, but I dare to ask for a double portion of your love!"

Praying the rosary first of all is a prayer of great spiritual expectation. Praying the rosary we meet with Jesus and His Mother, the Queen of Heaven and Earth, the Mediator of all Graces who triumphed over evil and is a fountain of various consolations and graces. The more we become aware of whom we meet during the rosary, the greater will be our expectation and it will be matched only by Mary's joy in seeing it. A soul who enters prayer with an expectation of meeting a loving God is predisposed to receive and mediate graces from God. This state of soul has achieved the faith necessary for the fulfilment of prayers.

From day to day we should discover what we can expect during our encounter with Our Lady in the rosary never forgetting that the encounter is taking place in God.

We should never forget either that petitioning through the rosary is just one aspect too. The rosary is God's celebration, our gratitude and our rendering to God the honour that is rightfully His, and acknowledging the holiness of Mary. It is also a school for life which teaches us how to walk in holiness and humility.

When I am speaking of expectation, firstly I am referring to it in its spiritual dimension: Man as the creation of God, as the son - who awaits and expects to enter a communion with the Creator, the Father, the Redeemer, the Saviour. Since I have been reborn in the Spirit, my soul is in a constant longing to be united with this Creator in prayer. My soul simply *desires* to be with God like the deer that yearns for streams of spring water.

Elijah's Spirit

Paul the apostle writes that he prays both with his spirit and with his mind (See 1 Cor 14.15). The prophet Elisha deeply desired and received Elijah's spirit as his heritage. We also saw that Saint Teresa of the Child Jesus also wanted the same thing. Elijah was a man that God was using. He didn't let his spirit limit the work of God. He was full of expectation and God used him. He knew God personally. The law of God (which is simply love) was woven into his reflections. Elisha knew this and that's why he asked for as much as he could receive. Elisha knew that Israel would not have the same protection and leadership from God anymore, if Elijah's spirit, the same one that Elijah had doesn't come alive again. God fulfilled Elisha's prayer. If only more people would pray like Elisha (See 2 Kings 2.1-14).

We know that the lives of the apostles really only started to change when Jesus breathed His Spirit into them. Jesus' Spirit is the Holy Spirit and at the same time He is the Father's Spirit just as the Creed tells us: the Spirit- *who proceeds from the Father and the Son and with the Father and the Son is worshipped and glorified.* Their way of apprehending and understanding Christ's good news had radically changed. They no longer sought the kingdom of this world, but rather the kingdom of heaven. After that on Pentecost, they received a power necessary to announce the Gospel so that God could confirm their words with signs and miracles (see Mk 16,20).

If we examine the beginning of Acts, we will notice in Peter's speech before Pentecost, the apostles knew exactly what to expect .i.e. what to pray for. The Apostle Peter not only discerned Jesus as the Messiah from Old Testament Scripture, but he recognized the prophecy that Judas would betray Him and would need to be replaced with a new apostle (see Acts 1.15-20). The most learned scripture scholars of that time weren't able to recognize this. And Peter wasn't even slightly bewildered after the descent of the Holy Spirit and the manifestation through the gift of tongues. On the contrary, he efficiently explains to the Jews what has happened, because together with the other apostles, he truly received the Spirit which illuminated his mind to understand what was written in the Old Testament (See Lk 24.45). The apostles had a rough idea too what to expect by the power of the Holy Spirit before they received it because they had someone by their side who had already had an experience of the outpouring the power of the Holy Spirit. We know from the scriptures that when Mary conceived Jesus, then the Holy Spirit's power came over her. Through this we can see that the Holy Spirit is the one who brings changes into our lives.

Elijah's spirit knew and understood God. That is why he was so strong in God's power. Elisha knew this and that's why he prayed to obtain the same ability in the spirit. What Elisha really received was the same gift as the apostles - the Holy Spirit who enlightened his mind and spirit so he could continue to do what Elijah had done. That is what we need too. Jesus' Spirit so that we can see the world with His eyes and understand it with His heart, to understand the Scriptures and the teaching of the Church and that we 'put on' the power of the Holy Spirit so that we would be able to witness to the same world the truth of the Gospel and to intercede for mercy for it.

I am a witness that it is very possible even today to experience the same thing. And today, just like the apostles, we contact and listen to Jesus (especially through the Word and the Eucharist) but without the Holy Spirit, we cannot really meet Him as our personal Saviour and Redeemer.

At the last supper, Jesus himself carried out the transubstantiation of the bread into His body and the wine into His blood and gave the apostles communion. But if we look a little closer we will see that that Communion, (which in itself is a powerful fount of strength of the living God,) because they weren't open, it couldn't be recognized in its fullness. His three best and favourite apostles couldn't even keep vigil with him a few hours later in the garden of Gethsemane. In fear they all abandoned him that evening. It is obvious that back then, they were still unable to discern in the spirits the reality of Jesus' body and blood in the Eucharist.

But after they received the Holy Spirit, which Jesus breathed into them, they became fearless. One hundred and twenty of them gathered everyday for prayer. Even though one hundred and twenty people gathering daily in the same place were very conspicuous, they weren't afraid anymore. In the same way, we cannot recognize or spiritually discern Jesus in the Eucharist or the Word without the Holy Spirit. When we are unable to discern in spirit, we prevent ourselves receiving blessings even though we hear and read the Word and we receive the Eucharist. This was the main reason why many in the Corinthian Church were weak and ill and some were even dying (see 1 Cor 11.27-30). It is also one of the main reasons for today's miseries, both of the body and of the soul. God gave us the food from which we have to live: the Eucharist and the Word - if we do not discern the risen Christ in these realities, we will miss many of the fruits which Christ has prepared for us in those Sacraments. There are many blessings in the Eucharist and the Word, the moment they become our prayer, i.e. our personal encounter with the risen Christ. Then they become our joy. Prayer always encloses us into God, and for that reason it must be both our joy and our fountain of life.

How to Pray

The apostles asked Jesus to teach them how to pray after they had already spent a lot of time with Him. Wasn't that a little strange? They were all people of faith. They all had prayer experience. Some of them had been true 'sons of the law' all their lives and prayed regularly. Some had first been John's disciples and had an even stronger experience of prayer. Others had for a certain period of their life distanced themselves from the Lord, for example Matthew, the tax collector. But even he would have had some experience of prayer. At that time no young man could have come of age as sons of the Law if they didn't know the Law and the prayers which had to be prayed as an integral part of the Law.

Isn't it interesting that the evangelist records the specific moment and situation when the apostles asked Jesus to teach them to pray. It happened after they had developed some personal experience. First Jesus sent them out to evangelize as the twelve and then as seventy. The gospel tells of how the apostles were successful in proclaiming. They performed various miracles, healed the sick and - what stood out most - were very successful in casting out demons. Even Jesus showed His contentment with their work. In this we can see that their prayers achieved a lot. When they failed with the boy who suffered from epilepsy, their enthusiasm quickly deflated. It was then that they realized that prayer is not primarily a means to obtain something from God. They realized that in the first place, it is continual joy and peace in the heart that you get from God in prayer. In other words, you get *God himself*. This is something that the majority of Christians don't understand.

Observing Jesus they realised that he prayed differently. They saw that another dimension of prayer exists distinct from the one they were familiar with. Reading the gospel to the end, it's easy to see that their prayer life didn't change for the better even after Jesus taught them to pray, by teaching them the Our Father. They learned the words, but they didn't learn how to pray. They couldn't pray in the way Jesus told them because they still were not filled with the Holy Spirit. Even though he knew that they were unable to fully comprehend, he still taught them because he knew that they would understand everything afterwards (see Jn 14.26).

How did Jesus pray? He prayed with his whole soul, not just His mouth. His prayer was a sincere (complete) encounter with His Father. God would like to encounter us completely. When we encounter God we encounter Him in our completeness. God doesn't listen just to our mouth, but also to our hearts. Only when we are completely in harmony with ourselves, can we meet God the way He truly is. We will try to explain in the simplest possible way so that we can comprehend the essence of prayer and the '*The rosary - prayer of my spirit*' because it is a prayer we pray with our whole being. Before we pray we have to bring our spirit in harmony with Him, whom we are turning to in prayer, and with what we are expecting from God in prayer. We'll start with our relationship with God.

Our Father

Let's begin with the prayer that Jesus taught us Himself. Try to imagine the situation when Jesus was in front of His apostles or in front of a crowd on a mount (see Lk 11.1-4; Mt 6.5-15) delivering this prayer to His heavenly Father. His mouth was pronouncing the word: *Father* In what pose was His body at that moment? What dictated to the position of His body? Do we always pray in the same body position? Or does the position of the body depend on the situation in which we find ourselves, the place where we pray, the content of the prayer that is in our hearts at that moment, our temporary emotional mood or any other factors?

We can pray kneeling, standing, sitting, lying down. Our hands can be raised folded, outspread, or our palms rested downwards. They can be still or we can wave them around and clap them to show God how much we like to praise Him with our whole soul. You might notice that when we are really concerned about our communication with God we do it spontaneously and with the whole body.

For instance, when someone close to us is in danger, our hands and body pray together with our words and heart. Maybe we can even recall instances when we raised our hands up, nearer to God. Can anyone say at a moment like that, that our position wasn't in keeping with the practice of prayer? Praising is prayer too. Can we really praise God if we only use our voices or is it not completely normal to use our bodies as well, if it is in our character? Let us pray with the whole being *but all things should be done decently and in order* (See 1 Cor 14.40).

It must have been that way when Jesus prayed on the mount before a crowd of people teaching them the Our Father. He must have extended his hands outwards and gently raised them with His palms turned upwards. We can imagine though, that His body position was different when He prayed on the Mount of Olives, or when He withdrew into seclusion to be alone with the Father - which was often.

The moment He said the word Father, His thoughts were united with that word and He wasn't thinking of anything else; He was completely focused on the Father. I believe that the majority of us focus our minds on our heavenly Father when we say those words too. If we mess it up at the start by not even thinking of what we're saying, how can our prayer become joy? So too if we are saying the words too fast, our minds can't even penetrate the meaning. The rhythm of '*The rosary - prayer of my spirit*' should be adjusted to our mind, giving ourselves time to think of the meaning of the words. Sometimes our prayer can even start and finish in the same instant, because it brings us before God's throne. Sometimes the spirit enables us to pray it at a normal pace, and still simultaneously take in every word and let those words seep into our souls from where they can bring fruit.

What happens in our soul when we say the Father's name? The soul is an immortal part of the human being created by God at the moment of conception. It is a part of the human being that can be discerned by the way we think, our mood, feelings and attitudes. The individuality of each soul develops from conception. It inherits characteristics through the parenting we experience. It also develops through the experiences that it had in relating to its surroundings and to itself. On the basis of information which our spirit has received, (the spirit is a part of the self which - amongst other things - unconsciously communicates with its surroundings and interprets what is happening around us, but is also capable of communicating with God) the soul reaches its own conclusions and attitudes and in that way forms its own personality. But even after baptism, the effects of original sin are there and learning from the catechism of the Catholic Church, we know that the two largest after effects are ignorance (of God) and the feeling of abandonment by God. So we can only imagine how many misguided attitudes, feelings, desires and emotions cloud the soul. Let's go back to the Our Father, and analyse what exactly is our soul saying during prayer.

Even though most of the time we are not conscious of what we are praying, we can be sure that God who is listening to us is *very* aware of what our soul is praying at that moment. Let us always ask questions and look for answers!

What does our sense of reason allow us to accept about God our Father? What is registered in our computer-like sense of reason about the Father? Do we have to pray to Him or to Jesus or to both? Where exactly is our Father? Is He only in heaven or is He near us? Is He in us through christening? What exactly do we know about our Father and how much do we desire to know the truth? What is our attitude regarding God as our Father?

Through life we've probably gathered up information and experience to establish a certain attitude or way of relating to Him. Even though we're not aware of it, when we come before God in prayer we have a definite 'attitude' with which we enter every prayer regardless of whether we approach Him directly or through Jesus or Mary or any other 'residents' of heaven! I've already said that every prayer takes place in God so he can always see our attitude. Unfortunately too many Christians blame God for many of the bad things that happened to them during their lives. Many see Him as a merciless Old Testament judge or at least someone who can help but won't.

On one occasion I held a talk about inner healing for about three and a half thousand people. I asked them how many of them during prayer truly love our heavenly Father and how many of them turn to Him with love and joy in their prayers. About ten people put their hands up. Ten people out of a few thousand had a correct inbuilt attitude towards our heavenly Father. Even though the Church and the Bible teach us that our heavenly Father loves us immensely and that His true name is love, only a small number of Christians really believe it and have that correct inbuilt attitude.

What is my attitude? Is it not strange that we admit to being Christian and yet we do not believe in one of the most important truths of the Christian life? Is it possible to be the Father's son and at the same time not believe it? Can we really be Christian without that inbuilt attitude telling us that our heavenly Father created us out of love and that His love is never-ending? It should tell us that we can and should always lean on Him. Let's imagine that He isn't Love, in fact He is the opposite! Our lives would have no sense. They would be filled with fear and distrust, knowing that our heavenly Father doesn't love us. And unfortunately, many commit suicide because they never found out that God our Father loves them immensely.

What are my feelings towards my heavenly Father? Quite often we don't realize that a feeling exists even though we are not aware of it. Feelings well up in our soul so our prayers are 'coloured through' with them - and we are not aware of it. Love and trust are the feelings we should have when we are appealing to our heavenly Father. Instead we often feel fear, indifference, aversion even condemnation and hatred. How will God see our prayer if we say our prayers without love or trust or any sort of filial association or sense of belonging? We must suppress the emotions brought on by our petitions (eg. fear of death when suffering with an incurable illness) and find the proper disposition within ourselves and nurture love and trust towards the one to whom we pray. When our trust in God our Father outweighs our fear (of death for example) we will be very close to receiving an answer to our prayers from God.

How much do I wish to be in the Father's company? How much time am I prepared to put aside for Him? Have I got the will and the desire to get to know Him better or am I avoiding situations where I could be closer to Him? Do I sincerely wish from the bottom of my heart to encounter my heavenly Father during prayer or am I just praying because I think I have to, because the Church asks us to and because I am afraid that God will turn against me. Do I willingly strive, with the will of my soul i.e. free will to spend more time with the Word, so that I may become better acquainted with the Father? How often do I pray the Our Father?

As soon as we start asking ourselves these questions and looking for an answer, the sooner our soul will change its attitude towards our heavenly Father. Our soul is very complex and in need of salvation. A resurrection or a new life is needed. We have to die to our wrong attitudes towards God so that a resurrection (the correct attitude) can take place. To die means to see that our attitude was wrong and sinful, then repent and seek forgiveness. Forgiveness on its own will not bring final changes. Through forgiveness we knock down our old attitude. If we are to truly repent and decide to change, a new attitude has to be built up. Many get to the stage of repenting and forgiveness but never actually move on to establishing a new attitude. They simply let the old wrong attitude re-establish itself and go back to the start.

If we want to change, we need the Holy Spirit. He is the only one who can enlighten us to get an insight into the truth, free us from the old attitude and construct the new one. That new attitude is not static; it constantly renews and improves itself as we improve and as our knowledge of God grows.

Often I read the Bible with the intention of knowing and loving God better. In that way my love for Him will be less imperfect. Through God's Word, I also want to get to know myself. I want to be more capable of recognizing that love, accept it and direct it to my fellow men. Sometimes though, I read the Bible with a concrete question for the Holy Spirit. Recently I desired to get to know the Father better through the Word. I was inspired to read the Gospel according to John. On reaching the middle, I realized that in the Gospel of John, he is continually referring to the Father with exceptional care and gentleness. I noticed that Jesus often utters the Father's name. I made an effort to count how many times the Father is mentioned in the Gospel of John. I was amazed to find that it was way over a hundred. Up until then I hadn't understood that the Gospel of John was in fact a gospel of Love. Now I understood what relationships that that Love is about. In other words, that Gospel clearly tells us of the reciprocal Love of the three Divine persons and how that love is directed towards creation, towards man. It has though, a specific angle, a depth of understanding of the love of the Father. If we prayed to the Holy Spirit to reveal the Love of God to us in the Word, we would be taken on the most incredible journey that we can imagine. Entering the presence of God, we are actually entering the area, the realms of the spirit. When we become deeply conscious of the presence of the Holy Spirit in our own inner self and implore His help in order to enthrone God at the centre of our hearts, and accept Jesus as our Saviour and Redeemer, then the Holy Spirit makes Himself known in His fullness. The Holy Spirit enlightens our soul and helps it to change. When we are praying, if we direct our spirit towards God and quell the negative attitudes of our spirit, we will then start to discern the voice of God who will bring changes in us. In prayer we come before God and raise up our spirits, saying *no* to all that is negative in our spiritual attitude towards Him. Little by little we come to see our life's experiences through God's Word and not in the way *life* has taught us to see them or through the wisdom of this world. Since the Bible has told us that the ruler of this world is Satan, (1 John) we often accept godless and worldly attitudes and thoughts and sometimes even the devil's thoughts as the truth. The Word of God teaches us that we have a daily duty to re-shape our mind so that we can be true children of God. (Eph 4.23)

In our prayer encounter then, we can often come with the wrong attitude towards the Person to whom we are praying. Often too, we come with the wrong attitude with regard to *what* we are praying for. The word 'wrong' here is misleading; perhaps the word 'immature' or 'imperfect' would be better. In so far as we don't notice the imperfection of our attitude, but remain entrenched in I t- then it is *wrong*. In so far as we have begun to reflect on our attitude and are beginning to change it - it doesn't matter that we are only starting to change - if we are trying, then this is the extent to which we are no longer wrong. It is not even sinful; it is simply immature, like the behaviour of small children. When we have advanced in building a better attitude, it can still happen that we fall, although less often than before, we can then say that our attitude is imperfect. Every way in which we relate to God that isn't enlightened by the Holy Spirit we can say that it's false, and those that are enlightened, true. Let's reveal the false ones and 'enlighten them' so that they become true:

At the mention of the Father's name in the *Our Father*, we can detect what our attitude is. We are praying for the hallowing of His name, for the Kingdom to come, for the fulfilment of His will, for the fulfilment of our daily material and spiritual needs, for the forgiveness of our sins and the sins of others, for the protection against temptation and to be delivered from all evil. With regard to all these requests, our soul has a definite disposition or attitude. Maybe we are conscious of this, maybe not. When we recite these requests, we don't just bring the words, we bring the disposition of the heart.

The whole point of the 'The rosary - prayer of my spirit' is that we pray it with the right attitude. At the beginning, we pray it imperfectly, but our disposition will mature fast. In this, I would like to help you change your attitude, stance or disposition with regard to the Father. I will teach a method whereby we can analyze and change what's lacking in our attitude:

After I was re-born in the spirit, I built up a very good relationship with two of the Divine persons; the Holy Spirit and the Son. Towards Mary, my disposition had been completed many years before. I thank Mary for bringing me to a personal encounter with her Son and the Holy Spirit, at the request of the Father in His love for me. It was a few years later during meditation that a Bible quotation came unexpectedly to me. I knew it was the Holy Spirit talking. This was the piece of scripture I heard:

(Jn 6.44)
No one can come to me unless drawn by the Father who sent me.

In that same instant I knew that my relationship with my heavenly Father wasn't good. I realized that He first loved me. He was the one who brought me to Mary and through her to her Son Jesus. The Father had created me and moulded me in the palm of His hand. At my christening He had accepted me as His beloved son. I started telling Him how much I loved Him with my whole heart and how sorry I was that I didn't see these things before. Since then my heart has been filled with love towards the Father and my prayers to Him are characterized with the expectation of His love.

I began reflecting about my attitude to the Father. There's no problem when we reflect on *Jesus'* love for us - we know He suffered a terrible torture and died for us. When we contemplate the tortures He undertook, in spite of His innocence, that love is easily comprehended. When we read about the healings and deliverances, it's not hard to believe in His love towards the suffering. He was even saddened when His native brethren rejected those miraculous healings. And even though He was like us in the flesh, He opted for poverty to show His love for the poor. How can we fail to love Him? The Bible tells us that His love towards us is unchanging, that He is with us today and up to the end of the world. (See Heb 13.8 and Mt 28.20) This is a love which has really demonstrated itself. But the Father?

We might think that our Father didn't suffer for us-that He even abandoned Jesus in his agony in the Garden of Gethsemane. How wrong can we be!

Most of us have children. Let's imagine that we are together with our child and others in a war situation and one of us has to be killed so that the whole group can be saved. I believe that every one of us would volunteer our own lives rather than see our child be killed because we know that it would affect us much more than our own death. Can we imagine the Father's pain, not just at the moment of His torture, but during the whole period when He was being rejected officially by Israel, they were rejecting Him through His Son. In order for the sacrifice to be perfect, the Father could not be with Jesus on the Cross. But that just added to the Father's pain. This is the way that God gave His only Son so that anyone who believes in Him would not die, but have eternal life.

Jesus didn't do anything that His Father did not allow Him to do. All of Jesus' works have their origins in the Father. (Jn 5.19-20) Luke's gospel tells us that the power (which was love) of the Lord was with Him to heal (Lk 5.17). It was the Father's wish that His Son would be born in a stable so that the most sorrowful people of this world know that their heavenly Father loves them most! When we reflect deeply on this, we will realize that we don't have a correct relationship with the Father. If we think just a little about it, we will realize that we didn't build up much of a relationship towards our Father, not owing to any fault on His part, but out of our own prejudice, and because of our own ignorance, our attitudes are misguided. The fact is the image we have of our heavenly Father is conditioned by our personal earthly father. No-one's earthly father is perfect and so we cannot have a correct picture of our Father in heaven. Although those who received love from their earthly fathers in childhood are much better able to understand God as Father. Still we cannot accept love if we come to Him with our hearts closed. Our love opens the heart so that we can recognize and accept the Father's love. Let's pray continually to the Father with confidence to draw as many souls to the Son so that they can be saved!

What about our attitude to the intentions we are praying for? The whole point of man's being on the earth points to an encounter with God and growing in love towards Him i.e. to merit heaven. Even though this is the main truth of our faith, not many pray to go to heaven. It is even difficult to find a prayer which concretely specifies a request to go to heaven. This is quite unusual. Orally we can recite a prayer to God to go to heaven, but the question is; what is our soul praying for at that moment. Remember that God firstly listens to the voice of the soul! Let's analyse our attitude towards heaven, the same way as we did towards our Father - asking as many questions as possible and looking for the answers.

What exactly do we know about heaven? How do we imagine it? What do we expect from heaven? Who is eligible and how do they go to heaven?

Preaching about it I like to ask questions. The first one is:

Will we have our own free will in heaven?

Man is very afraid of losing his personal freedom. Just think how many people gave their life for freedom. And yet no-one was freed except through Jesus Christ. It is unbelievable how seldom I manage to get an answer to the question whether we will have our own free will in heaven, because people rarely wonder about that. It is amazing that people hardly ever reflect about the most important questions of human existence. Out of the people questioned, very few answered that they believed that in the other world, they have their own free will. But the truth is pleasantly surprising- in heaven they will be much freer than they are now! We know that angels had their free will and some of them decided to rebel against God. God did not take their right to choose away. They chose and erred. What's significant for us though is that they were able to choose. We as the future residents of God's kingdom of heaven will have the same free will and will be able to decide to do as we wish, even though we, unlike the angels will not be able to sin. Because of that we will keep our free will and be perfect. The second question I ask is:

Apart from 'looking at God' what will we be doing? Will it be boring?

Being in God's presence, it will never be boring. Finally, arriving in heaven we will have the chance to voluntarily meet many people who got to heaven before us. Some of them are familiar and people who are dear to us, but most of them we don't know. We will be able to communicate voluntarily or simply be brother or sister to so many good and interesting people who will respect us as equals. Seeing that God's kingdom has a very specific structure (remember the various choirs of angels) it's more than likely that we will fit in somewhere into that structure - which will have its own characteristics. Observing babies, we can see how they cry for the affection of their parents. At least my own children when they were babies wanted to be held and hugged endlessly. Raising all four of them, I don't think any of them were ever 'bored' when they were held in our arms. We will arrive in heaven as newly born babies! If there is one sure thing it is that we won't suffer boredom in heaven. On the contrary, it will be very interesting and exciting.

Not long ago I held a short seminar for a Catholic Charismatic prayer group with a long history of charismatic experience. In keeping with the theme I both spoke and prayed with practically every member of the group. Amongst other questions, I asked them who they thought they'd meet in heaven. They answered that they would meet Jesus, Mary, all the angels and saints and some family members or close friends. Not one of the thirty people questioned had a prepared answer. In fact they needed time and reflection to be able to answer. Only one person answered that she would meet a huge number of people who had reached heaven before her. On reflection, we see that this is a sign that the faithful don't think much about heaven, even though heaven is what we should be directing our lives towards. At the same time we are so self-absorbed, that we don't even recognize the practical implications of needing to save so many souls around the whole world. Only he or she who prays with love for the salvation of the world has that in-built correctly positioned attitude regarding the need of mediation prayer. To the question who we will meet in heaven, they will always reply to the infinite number of God's children who we can hardly wait to meet to share eternity together. In heaven there will be brothers and sisters from other cultures, life experiences, times etc. If we show God now that we are truly joyful to be part of heaven, where we will have a chance for joint eternal life with an infinite number of people, where everyone has their own amazingly interesting life story, I am sure that God will open the door of heaven even wider! The third question is:

Will we keep our own personality?

People are really afraid of losing their personalities. If God gave us the opportunity to switch places with any other person of our own choice in our earthly life, it's very likely that we wouldn't want to change with anyone. I have seen people with difficult life problems, those who are very ill; who are misunderstood and not accepted in their surroundings and still, no one wants to exchange places. We love ourselves immensely and we're not even conscious of it. We know that it's not possible to exchange with some one else but thinking about it will give us answers to some important question. When we study a Christian psychology of man, we realize that not many recognize their own personality. The personality of a Christian is the personality of a child of God. It is wise to have this in mind when we are leaving this world. That knowledge is enough to bring us immense joy and liberate us from any fear. The more we suffer with complexes - lets take a complex of unworthiness or the feeling of having been abandoned, or the feeling of guilt - the less we are free in our true personality. Imagine what a joy it will be when we arrive in heaven and recognize the worthiness of our own personality which due to the circumstances of this world we were unable to see. That will be our first and greatest joy. So the answer is, of course we will have our own personality in heaven, but there we will have an awareness of it's infinite value and greatness.

How much do we desire heaven in the depths of our hearts? How much do we pray that we will reach heaven? How much are we prepared to sacrifice here in this worldly life for heaven? How much are we concerned that others too, besides ourselves actually reach heaven? Are the answers that lie in our hearts at this moment in keeping with the teachings of the Bible, and with the teachings of our faith? If not, remember that we could even die today. What then? Can a just and objective God take us to heaven if in the depths of our hearts, with our lives and our attitudes we have never shown Him or ourselves that that is what we want? Can He give us the greatest of treasures, if we don't yearn for Him? Can any of our 'good deeds' compensate for the fact that in our heart of hearts we never yearned for heaven even though Jesus gave His life, so that we, on this earth could have a foretaste of heaven and that after death we would have it eternally? Will God in the moment of our deaths not respect the free will of our hearts which has decided that we are not really 'pushed' about going to heaven nor do we want to be with Him? You answer yourself.....

I once asked a group why they would like to go to heaven. Hardly anyone had an answer. One woman said that she'd like to go there so that she wouldn't have to spend eternity with 'bad people' down in hell! How unfortunate it is that so many of us Catholics think the same way.

When we talk, read or think about heaven, what do we feel-desire, hope, love or indifference? Maybe we feel fear? For many people, heaven is just a slightly better alternative to hell! How many Catholics have I heard that from!

If we put our thoughts, will and emotions together, we will see that we have a definite attitude or disposition towards heaven. If we were asked about it, would we be able to define it concisely? By it we can clearly see to what extent we know God, or perhaps it would be better to say, 'how much we love God?' Comprised within that attitude is also the strength of our conviction about what the best way to get to heaven is and what sort of people go there. The general consensus among Catholics is that it is *people without sin* that go to heaven or *those who managed to confess before death.* God didn't create us just to be in peace with Him, although it is a basic pre-requisite. He created us to know Him, to love Him and by doing that, to pave the way to heaven. If we have no sins, that doesn't mean that we don't have a sinful 'character' or 'personality'- and it certainly doesn't indicate that we love God. But in so far as we have 'sins' that is the extent to which we consolidate our attitude as sinners. If we do not love God, we sin against His greatest and most important commandment. But even those who *love* God can sin and make mistakes, not because they are sinful characters or bad people (the classic archetypes are the adulterer, the killer, the thief) but rather because of the weakness of the flesh. Lets comprehend once and for all that we cannot go to heaven unless we really want to and unless we love God. The ruler of heaven is our Father and we can only go there as His adopted child, who lives in this world instead of His only Son. Remember the testimony of the woman whose Son and husband were murdered? I must admit that I am really grateful for Purgatory, which for many opens the door to heaven. Without it they would be irretrievably lost!

If our attitude to heaven is not 'in order', let's repent and decide to change right away. Reflect, read, meditate and change your attitude to heaven. Begin with these words of St. Paul;

> (1 Cor 2.9)
> *Neither eye has seen nor ear has heard nor has the human heart conceived of what God has prepared for those who love Him.*

God's Will

Very often, ignorance of God's will prevents us from making progress in prayer. Ignorance of God inevitably causes ignorance of His will. In my book *Charisma of Faith*, I already wrote about this, but since it is inextricably linked with the theme of prayer, I cannot avoid pointing out some facts.

The Bible talks to us about God's will for us, about what God wishes for all of us and what he appointed for all of us. The good that He intends for us, we can call blessings, the evil a curse. The basis of God's will for our lives is that He created us so that we can meet Him, so that we will love Him and thereby go to heaven. We can then conclude that whatever brings us to a deeper knowledge of God and a deeper bond with His love *is* His will for our life. If things are happening to us that are drawing us away from Him and His love, it is not in God's plan for us. That conclusion however is not one hundred percent correct: The Bible and the Church teach us that, in every situation in our lives, God can turn every evil to good for those who love Him. It is so good to know that whatever happens to us in our lives, He is the one thing we can count on. Every good or evil in our lives, He can actually use to bind us even closer to Him and His love. We too can use every good or evil in our lives to bind ourselves closer to Him or to distance ourselves from Him. One thing is certain, He promised to be with us to the end of the world and that He would do His part to make sure that we are blessed. It is up to us to recognize His help, to accept it and to use it to make ourselves holy. God lets us decide whether we want to be 'blessed' or 'cursed'.

During a seminar on one occasion a woman approached me and said that she had a vision during prayer which concerned me. When she said that it concerned the time of twenty years from now, I gladly let her tell me what God had shown her. In the vision she saw me happy, after one of the seminars; I was sitting alone and saying "That is what I wanted". It was a very short vision, but it was very clear. I was busy with the seminar the following day so I hadn't got time to think right away about it or about what it could mean. On my way home I began to ask myself what God wanted to say with that. It was good to know that I would be alive in twenty years time and that I would be constant in announcing the Good News and I would even be happy! I was grateful to God for that. Was it because of what had happened during the seminar that I was really happy? (The lady had said that she knew that I had just finished a seminar in the vision.) I began wondering what I would really like to happen at the seminars. I could think of so many answers and none of them took precedence over the others.

I had to ask myself in general what the most important thing in my life was. I asked myself if God granted me one wish, what it would be. It had to be so great that I wouldn't change my mind later on and think that I'd asked for the wrong thing - that what I'd really wanted was something else. God would further fulfil my wishes, but none of them would be as big as the one I'd thought of as the most important one. I slowly began to realize that God really does ask that of each one of us, but many of us Christians answer it without thinking deeply, while the rest of us don't know what we would say. Those people who have prepared a good answer are very rare.

If a person admits that they cannot answer that question clearly, it means that he or she is plodding his way through life, but doesn't have a clear destination. From our conception to our mortal death, our life is a journey. That journey often turns into a real race. The beginning is our conception, and the destination is our heart's desire. But what if we really don't know what we want to happen? It became very clear to me that God wanted me to choose the destination of the journey of my life. One intelligent man, a long time ago asserted that the direction is always more important than the speed arriving to the goal. If we reflect a little deeper, we will see that it is good to know where we wish to go. The problem is that we can go to hell even though we don't want to, but to get to heaven we really have to want it! If we have many different goals, all of equal intensity, it is quite likely that we will never reach the destination that God's Providence has prepared for us.

Not long ago, I held a lecture for a group of clerics, most of whom were Parish Priests. I asked them two questions: What is the goal of their life and what is the goal of their parishioners. I presumed that all those who had 'discerned' the goal of their life had it 'registered' both in their heads and in their hearts. I thought that they would spend their lives (both actively and contemplatively) in accordance with that goal. A Parish Priest too, who knows in his heart what is the best thing that God can give each individual parishioner (so that it is in accordance with the will of God for him/her) will direct his priestly activities to helping the flock entrusted to him, arrive at that goal. I believe that the starting point of this way of living is to testify to your beliefs in your everyday life. Secondly all prayer too would be a continuation of that goal and finally all his activities would be directed to that goal too. If the priest had found the goal, he should have understood its unspeakable value, both in his own life and in the life of every individual soul of those entrusted to him by God and the Church. Neither would he wait for the 'lost sheep' to find their own way home, but rather he will look for anyone who, for whatever reason had gone from the assurance of home.

Unfortunately, even Priests sometimes are without the joy of the knowledge of 'God's nearness' and this has implications for the whole flock. Whoever has had an experience of the outpouring of the Love of God on one or more occasions, can only fall in love with

God and his/her soul only desires heaven. In so far as this has not taken place, it is most probable that faith will just become a ritual, a tradition or a necessary means to ensure we don't end up in hell. It is true that from the many conversations that I have had with the faithful, the majority of them practice the faith out of a fear of ending up in hell rather than out of gratitude and love towards God. Sunday sermons are enough to show whether our Parish Priest yearns for God or whether he is just hoping to avoid hell. Whatever the attitude of his heart may be, let's decide to support him with our prayer so that his work is worthy both of his parishioners and of God.

Personally, I want the most of what God is offering me. I told Him, "My biggest wish is to be as close to Your throne as possible in eternity. That's why I want to learn more about Your love, the love that You showed me on the Cross and I would like to return it with my own love as best as possible. I am prepared to pay any price for that, because no price is too high for something like that. I want to aim my life in that direction. Will You please be by my side so that I arrive at my goal. I also wish it for my family and friends and for each soul that You God created. If my children have to pay with their life to achieve that goal, or if they have to go through a lot of suffering, I joyfully accept this from Your hands and I won't see it as 'having been abandoned'. Instead I will see it as the opposite - a sign of Your exceptional love. The only thing I wish for is that You open the eyes of my heart so that I can recognize your hand in everything!"

Not everyone in heaven is equally blessed, so it would be absurd not to accept the offer for the biggest possible blessing. I don't mean receiving authority for instance like Zebedee's sons, but what is God's will - as the will of every father who loves his children - that as many of his kids in eternity be very blessed (closer to him, to love him even more). The place beside God's throne will always be free for those that truly want to go there. Unfortunately, due to ignorance towards God, not many Christians wish for it. Most of them want to be as far away as possible from His throne! God's throne is His heart. In heaven everyone will desire to be as close as possible.

In that way I resolved what I wanted for eternity, but still there was the question what happened at the seminar in the vision. Whatever it was it filled me with great happiness. Not long after the incident, I had to lead a prayer and talk in a parish in Croatia. I had visited the Parish before and so it was announced and the plans were for great numbers of people to come, escorted by buses etc. I was really glad about all the arrangements especially the fact that the resident parish priest participated fully in everything and stressed that besides preaching he would take it upon himself to pray for the needs of all those present. That Sunday there was a huge turnout and that made me really happy. But it all took a strange turn: The Parish Priest was taken with the huge turn-out and decided to do the whole program by himself. I thought that this decision would be very good because through it his faith would deepen. However it would seem that the Holy Spirit doesn't always blow the way we want Him to and the whole encounter passed with much preaching and petitioning and very little action on behalf of the Holy Spirit. I didn't realize then that the priest hadn't yet experienced the problem that every evangelist must face: i.e. He must know how to switch himself "off" and switch Christ "on" for the duration of the service. It was only towards the end of his life that the apostle Paul manages to do this. He says that it is no longer him who lives, but Christ who lives in him. (see Gal 2.20) Evangelization is based on so much sacrifice. Whoever God calls to the service of evangelization must forget himself, and often his family and many things that he likes because he will no longer have time for them. If my evangelization has already cost me many crosses, then I would like it to be as fruitful as possible so that many people can be saved. The main obstacle is myself, and never God because it is His desire that as many souls as possible be saved.

I understood that at that seminar I would achieve a complete switching off of myself and a complete identifying with Christ so that those at the seminar would get a look exclusively at God because to Him belongs all the glory and that I put my trust in His mercy, and not as I often do, in my own faith. But what is more important is, that I understood that I would achieve this only because I would have really returned love for love - because love never seeks its self (1 Cor 13.5)

Let this testimony sink in for a while and think about the will of God!

The Blessed Virgin Mary

My whole life has been marked by a devotion to the Blessed Virgin Mary. Our parents had taught us from childhood to pray Our Lady's greeting (the Angelus) regularly, and to have trust in her intercession. And, as I mentioned earlier, my grandmother inspired me with an even stronger devotion to Our Lady. I can still remember a very clear dream in which Our Lady appeared to me. In it she promised me special help and protection throughout my life. She asked me to always have something blue on me to remind me of her. Today I can't remember a day that I haven't at least carried a blue handkerchief in my pocket. And a few years after that dream, when I was working with a team giving a Charismatic seminar in a Salesian church in Ljubljana, I recognized the image of Our Lady from my dream on the centerpiece of the church: it was Mary Our Help!

My real conversion (conscious change of life) began when I spent two days in Medjugorje in 1987. I didn't see or feel anything, but I can definitely say that everything changed in those two days in Medjugorje. After that my life took a completely different direction. That conversion was a bit like Mary's life; it went unnoticed, even though it was powerful and strong. It was as if I eventually gave into the love that had been seeping into my heart throughout the years. I believe that Mary becomes a real mother for many in Medjugorje. We can't see her, but we become spiritually aware of her presence and her leadership, which takes us down the best path to God. Medjugorje has brought millions of people to God, in many different ways. The majority of them have joined various church movements and some have even chosen a church vocation. Personally, I believe that Mary brought me to the Charismatic movement because she knew that I would fulfil my purpose in life in that way. We should be grateful that in our Church there are so many church movements. Today, there are over sixty acknowledged and many that are on their way to being acknowledged. Each of these movements is equally valuable because they can all bring people to God in their own way. Unfortunately most of our parishes cannot organize well for the faithful to be closely connected, so church movements are a good solution for those who wish to live their faith in a community - like atmosphere with other brothers and sisters.

Mary didn't only bring me to God and other worshippers but also to myself. I remember how I had always had problems with my name. I didn't like it, and no one at home, neither friends nor neighbours called me by my full name. They used some other version or some nickname. I didn't like it when someone called me *Josip*. Not long after my experience in Medjugorje I visited our National shrine of the Mother of God in *Marija Bistrica*. There after Mass I stayed in the church to meditate. From nowhere I heard a word spoken so beautifully in my heart; it was my name! Internally I began to cry and I knew that I was experiencing an inner healing from the wounds received because of my name. From then on, second only to the names of Jesus and Mary, my name became the nicest name for me. It was enough to hear the name spoken on Mary's lips to change everything!

Reading the Bible and meditating on the Word of God I experienced many revelations about God's love, but the majority of valuable revelations, I received during the prayer of the rosary.

Many times when praying for those in need; I didn't always trust that God would answer my prayers. But I always trusted that Mary would help in the best possible way in each individual circumstance. While praying for people who were under the influence of evil forces, I often experienced that demons feared and panicked at the concept of Our Lady!

I think that most Catholics know a fair bit about Our Lady, so I won't quote the Catechism of the Catholic Church, or the II Vatican Council documents, or any of the books that describe Our Lady so beautifully, although I do recommend them to anyone who really wants to cultivate a deep devotion to Our Lady. Instead, I want to touch on what will help to describe *'The rosary-prayer of my spirit'* better. I won't be very systematic because I merely want to inspire you readers to plunge into this immense treasure by reading, meditating and praying yourselves.

The mysteries of the rosary

We know that there are various mysteries that briefly describe the life of Jesus in the rosary. We have the joyful, sorrowful and glorious mysteries, and also the luminous mysteries. Depending on what part of the world you are in, the mysteries are brought into the rosary differently. I was taught to mention each mystery inside the Hail Mary after the word 'Jesus'. For e.g. "...and blessed is the fruit of your womb, Jesus, *to whom you gave birth* Holy Mary, Mother of God, pray for us..." I heard that Pope John Paul II prayed it in this way too and that made me really happy. In other parts of the world the mystery is mentioned after the Our Father, i.e. before the first Hail Mary. In many places you contemplate the mystery while praying the words of the Hail Mary, but the main aim of *'The rosary - prayer of my spirit'* is that during the Hail Mary you *don't* contemplate the mystery. During the rosary our thoughts are directed to the words that are said while praying. We become aware of the 'weight of meaning' of each word pronounced during the prayer. Every word carries with it all the characteristics of our personality and our spirit is immersed into the mystery, which itself is primarily of spiritual nature. With our mind we can be connected to the pronounced words while with our spirit we are immersed in the mystery that we are praying. You will see that it is not too complicated.

An important part of the *'The rosary - prayer of my spirit'* is the preparation that we carry out i.e. contemplating the mystery "beforehand" or even better said, "outside of the actual prayer", because we have to contemplate over the mystery when we have the chance to do so. In such a way we build our inner relationship towards each individual mystery. A relationship in 'registering' each mystery onto our own heart and understanding what is actually happening during the mystery. Secondly it is about the influence, which that individual mystery can have on us while praying it.

We will contemplate the various aspects of each mystery, but our main aim will be to perfect the relationship of our soul with the prayers of each individual mystery.

The first joyful mystery
– The Annunciation to Mary

What do we know about this mystery? Let's take a look at an excerpt from Luke's Gospel!

Lk, 1:26-38 – "In the sixth month, the angel Gabriel was sent by God to a town of Galilee called Nazareth, to a virgin engaged to a man whose name was Joseph, of the house of David. The virgin's name was Mary. And he came to her and, said, "Greetings, favoured one! The Lord is with you." But she was much perplexed by his words and pondered what sort of greeting this might be. The angel said to her, "Do not be afraid, Mary, for you have found favour with God. And now, you will conceive in your womb and bear a son, and you will name him Jesus. He will be great and will be called the Son of the Most High, and the Lord God will give to him the throne of his ancestors David. He will reign over the house of Jacob forever, and of his kingdom there will be no end..."

Mary said to the angel, "How can this be, since I am a virgin?" The angel said to her, 'The Holy Spirit will come upon you, and the power of the Most High will overshadow you, therefore the

*child to be born will be holy, he will be called
Son of God. And now your relative Elizabeth,
has also conceived a son in her old age, and this
is the sixth month for her who was said to be
barren. For nothing will be impossible with God.'
Then Mary said, Here am I the servant of the
Lord, Let it be with me according to your word.'
Then the angel departed from her.*

Let's analyse the text!

The angel Gabriel came to Mary six months after
John the Baptist was conceived. It happened in the
town of Nazareth which is located in Galilee. At the
time when the angel came, Mary was engaged to a man
from David's house (heritage), his name was Joseph.
The author of the Gospel points out to us that Mary
was a virgin.

The Angel entered and greeted her and wished
for her to be joyful because of the fact that she was
favoured by God - and God was with her. Mary was
frightened and began to wonder about the meaning of
the greeting. Church doctrine tells us that Mary was
filled with the Holy Spirit since her sinless conception.
God was closely bonded with Mary from the moment
of her conception. That bond was never broken; it was
further perfected. About Mary we can say that she was
completely in God and that God was in her. Coming
to her in prayer, in her and with her we meet our God
and the whole meeting is in fact carried out in God.

God gave us Mary so that it will be easier for us to get to Him! If we remember what Paul has in mind when he says that *he* is not alive but *God is* who lives in him, then we can imagine that that reality is even more true in Mary! Coming to Mary, in fact we are coming to God to whom she had opened up space to live in her! When we open the door for God to abide within us, then everyone who is destined to be blessed through us, no longer comes to us, but to the God who dwells within us, regardless of how He chooses to reveal Himself

Mary got a fright, but the angel assured her that there was no need to be scared because she had 'found grace with God'. In other words, the angel is telling her that God had fulfilled her prayer (You have found favour with God!). We can further conclude that Mary, as well as many other righteous people amongst the Jewish people, prayed for the arrival of the expected Messiah – the Saviour and deliverer of the Jewish people. From the angel's statement we can conclude that Mary was amongst those rare ones who prayed for the Messiah, who would free Israel from sin and spiritual death, but not from Roman occupation. Mary was expecting Isaac's Messiah who would bring the Kingdom of heaven to Israel and the whole world, but not a kingdom of this world, where Israel would be a privileged and ruling power.

The angel Gabriel furthermore gives clear knowledge to Mary that she will conceive and bear a son and give him the name Jesus. He will be great and he will be the Son of the Most High, he will reign to eternity. Mary therefore became completely aware of what would happen if she accepted.

Mary then asks a logical question: *"How will that be"* – Mary says to the angel – *"since I am a virgin?"* It is a logical question if Mary had previously (before the annunciation) together with Joseph decided to live in wedlock as virgins. In the actual question Mary let it be known that it would not be a problem if she had relations with her husband, but seeing that she decided to live as a virgin then there is a problem. On the other hand, if Mary had decided not to be a virgin after the marriage, she would surely not have asked such a question. Therefore, Mary wished to know how it would happen. From the Old Testament we know that it was prophesied that a virgin would conceive and bear a Son (see Is 7:14). Mary knew that, which is why she didn't ask if she would have to meet with her husband, but she had wanted to know how would a virgin (in this case her) conceive a child and furthermore stay a virgin. Remember that Zechariah did not ask the angel how Elizabeth would conceive a son, but rather he asked for a sign so that he could believe (see Lk 1.18-20)

The angel then answered her that the Holy Spirit would come upon her with the power of the Most High. Therefore her child will first be holy, then the Son of God. Even though Mary was already filled with the Holy Spirit, it was necessary again for the power of the Holy Spirit to come upon her. Remember the apostles that were filled with the Holy Spirit (Jesus had personally breathed into them), but for the mission of annunciation, the power of the Holy Spirit was needed from above – in the same way Mary had it to conceive Jesus! Through that we can see that Mary had received the Holy Spirit with its power before the apostles. The Holy Spirit is the One who gives Christians specific missions with the outpouring of His power!

I don't know how it looked for Mary and the apostles, but I know how it was for me. I can testify that it was truly the work of an incredible mighty power which filled me with a feeling of heaven, and at the same time, I felt it physically. It lasted for about half an hour and it was so powerful that the people present became frightened. I know that the power can come in various ways, but most often it comes through receiving various sacraments, where there is a true outpouring, even though the person who is receiving it may not feel anything emotionally or on a physical level.

Furthermore, the angel gives Mary information that Elizabeth her relative will conceive a son in her old age - even though she was barren - she was already six months pregnant. Take note here that Elizabeth was much older than Mary, and she could not have been her cousin as it is thought, but more likely a kinswoman, an aunt so John the Baptist was not the cousin of Jesus. The angel called her a relative. We have to ask ourselves why the angel spoke about Elizabeth to Mary! One of the reasons would be that he wanted Mary's faith to rise. By the angel's approach, also from further text in the Gospel, we can conclude that Mary knew Elizabeth. She knew that Elizabeth was an older woman, that she was barren and that she could have only conceived a child by the direct intervention of God. Seeing that Elizabeth accepted God's intervention in her old age to give birth to a son, it is logical that it would have helped Mary to offer her acceptance.

After Mary had heard about Elizabeth, she humbly accepted the mission that God had chosen for her, calling herself the servant of God. The angel then departed from her. Sometimes, in sermons we hear that Mary's crucial "fiat" was the most humble word that a person could say. But if we think better about it, was it not a little strange? That is, Mary who was young, almost an almost obscure Israelite girl, was offered to give birth to the Son of God – can there be a better offer for any human being than to become the Mother of God? How come Mary had not then mentioned her 'worthiness'? Maybe it would be more humble to say: "Lord you know that I am not worthy of such a great grace!" or something similar but in the same manner! But Mary did not say any such thing! Was Mary not lacking in humility then? By today's criteria, most Christians would say she was, but by the criteria of *God's Word* she definitely wasn't! Mary as a child of God, knew that she was worthy of receiving everything that God wished to give her, and it was precisely her humility that did not allow her to oppose God's wishes, no matter what they happened to be!

I experienced many times that when a person claims that God granted him/her an extraordinary gift or charism, others make objections saying that he/she is not humble because he/she is speaking about it openly. Remember how Mary proclaimed what God did for her in her canticle (see Lk 1:46-56)! We can not of course compare Mary conceiving Jesus with any other gift, but everything that comes from God, deserves our happiness and heartfelt praise from everyone in a prayer group! A prayer group should also know what God gives through specific people, so that we can support them in every way possible, especially in prayer.

Try to imagine what would have happened if Mary had answered the angel humbly by *today's understanding* of 'humility'. By it, we can not do anything because we are not worthy of anything! Would the angel try to reason with her and tell her that she is worthy and capable or would the same thing happen to her as to the father of John the Baptist?! When God wants to do something, he chooses precisely those who are incompetent in the eyes of this world (see 1 Cor 1.26-31); those who won't think that what God expects from them is something that is to *their* credit. For that reason, they will not question their personal worthiness or capability, but rather simply accept everything that God wishes to give or do through them: from the most difficult of trials or temptations to the greatest of glories!

The gift of uniting suffering with Jesus' suffering is most probably a greater spiritual gift than healing. I believe that more of God's grace is needed for someone to unite their sufferings in love with Jesus', than to believe that a healing has been granted. However when someone receives the charisma of healing, straight away the validity is questioned, while generally accepted to believe that we are all worthy of suffering, therefore no one asks that question. But if we suffer without the grace of the Holy Spirit, we have to ask ourselves have our sufferings the attributes of a gift (see 1 Cor 13.3)! From my own personal experience I can testify that there are a greater number of people who received healing from my prayers, and a lot less of those whose sufferings received meaning after uniting them with His. Let's ask ourselves is it necessary to be more worthy to receive healing or to accept suffering?!

When did Mary conceive Jesus? How much time had gone by from the annunciation to the conception? From the same Gospel we can easily draw a conclusion. Elizabeth at the time of the annunciation was already six months pregnant. Mary had visited her and stayed three months and returned home before John's birth (see Lk 1:56-57). Therefore we can conclude that from the moment of the annunciation to conception only a little time passed, maximum one month. Therefore, Mary had gone to Elizabeth straight after she had conceived Jesus.

The connection with the mystery

What does this mystery remind us of? Of course! It reminds us of our own conception, and the conception of every person on the Earth. It's true that the angels don't announce a large number of conceptions but the Bible or the Word of God speaks about every conception. The Bible tells us that God is the one who exhales the spirit and gives life. Through God's will we are all conceived and assigned for works of love that He has prepared in advance for us (see Eph 2.10). We were not all wanted or accepted in the same way from our earthly parents, but we can rest assured that someone did truly rejoice at the moment of our conception: it was our Creator, i.e. our God.

From the moment of conception, every person has a spirit which God has 'breathed' into him/her. That spirit even in infancy is just as 'capable' as that of an adult. The Bible tells us that we think with our spirit (see Eph 4.23). That is exactly what happens from the moment of our conception: with our spirit we communicate with our surroundings! God, at the moment of our conception, creates an eternal spirit. By the spirit we are designated for a supernatural life. Through it, our soul is enabled, by a pure gift, to be lifted to a communion with God. Differentiation of spirit and soul should not lead us to a dual conception of the soul, but rather, to a better explanation of its character, so that we can call it: a spiritual soul (see CCC 366-377). From the moment of our conception, at the level of the spirit, we are aware of the conditions in which we are conceived. Through the spirit, we are aware whether we were wanted or not by our father and mother.

So, on the basis of what our spirit acknowledges happening around us, our soul brings conclusions and forms attitudes. It is a continuing process throughout our whole life. The most intensive formation of the soul takes place up to our fifth and sixth year of life. Then our logical mind takes over the role of communication with our surroundings because our spirit often is not in harmony with human logic. Further on in our lives, we become aware of the existence of our spirit but we refer to it as a *sixth sense*. Many people throughout their lives have experiences of an infused 'knowledge' of things that are not really accessible to their minds. For instance the feeling that they have already been at a certain place, or the example of maybe driving a car when a word comes to your mind, and around the next bend you happen to see the word on a large advertisement on the side of the road. - Our spirit is much more capable then our mind. Unfortunately, most people do not know how to minister it in the correct way.

Therefore, on the basis of our experience during our conception, our soul brings specific conclusions and forms attitudes. It pertains to the essence of the soul to ordain attitudes toward the life situations in which we find ourselves. Maybe we didn't even notice that we developed personal attitudes about a lot of things that happened to us. Together with our attitudes come our emotions, and our will often proceeds from this. If we begin analysing our inner selves, we would see a combination of attitudes. Some are very important to us, and we are aware of them, while others, that are less important, we are not aware of. It is precisely those attitudes that constitute a good part of our soul, which shows itself through our understanding, will and emotion in the way we relate to the world around us. For this reason it is not possible to have two people in the world who are exactly the same. There are people who are similar to us to the extent that their attitudes towards individual issues are similar to ours.

After our sixth year, if attitudes are to change, it will mostly be in exceptional circumstances. It could happen during great emotional stress, whether positive or negative, or it can be the affect of spiritual forces; either that of the Holy Spirit through prayer, or that of evil spirits through contact with the occult, witchcraft or rationalization. Through that we can conclude that our whole life in many situations is conditioned by what happened to us during the first years of life. Our soul is in need of salvation and salvation of a soul does not only mean going to heaven. Firstly it must mean - to change the incorrect attitudes, because these take away our freedom to make correct decisions about many of life's situations. Incorrect attitudes, which usually result from bad experiences, block us from finding unity with God, which He, in his love, had predetermined for us (see CCC 27). Even though when our behaviour is different from most people around us, we believe it is a reflection of our freedom of choice - more often it is the result of the captivity of our soul. This in turn, is due to incorrect attitudes, which have their origins in the emotional wounds received in early childhood.

The problem is that we are born under the influence of original sin i.e. spiritually dead. It is the spirit of being separated from God's Spirit and we cannot enjoy God's closeness and protection like Adam and Eve during their stay in heaven. We are imprisoned by ignorance, suffering and the power that death holds over us and the tendency to sin.

This further means that our soul forms its attitudes on the basis of personal experience, on the apprehensions inherited from our parents, the influence of our surroundings, world views, ideologies or philosophies. Even though baptism wipes out original sin and brings man back to God, the after effects stay and continually provoke us on our spiritual battle. Hence, the transformation of our souls becomes a long term process where the emphasis is put on our free will through which God's grace can work on us and bring healing and liberation (cf. CCC 405). God gives us the chance to participate in our own transformation and sanctification with our own free will. This is what he calls us to (cf. CCC 302).

I will tell you a true story, an example of this help so that we can easily understand how it can take place. I will change some unimportant details to protect the identity of the person who I am speaking about.

Nicholas was a married man in his forties. With his wife and son he lived in the house of his wife's parents. His problem was that he – when he was in company – had to seriously avoid alcohol, because after a few glasses he would become very 'strange', telling everyone how no one in the world loves him. He would feel completely abandoned by everyone he lives with. He could not cope with the idea that his wife and son didn't love him, so he would wake up in the morning and leave for work before anyone would wake up. He would return home when he would feel sure that everyone had gone to sleep. He didn't know why he was like that nor did his family with whom he lived. Even though he was normal in everything else and a healthy person, he was very unhappy due to the feeling of having been abandoned by his nearest and dearest. One day he packed his bags and without a word of explanation left his wife and son. After a few months he decided to attend my Charismatic meeting. The exact theme of the meeting was: inner healing and liberation. He felt that this could be his problem. He cried out to God and during the prayer for inner healing and liberation God healed him showing him the root of his problem. What did he show him?

As a small child he became very sick and the doctors did not give him any hope of being healed. He was lying in the contagious section of the hospital, which meant not even his parents were able to visit him. His mother decided to do something. She made a vow to Our Lady that she would made a daily pilgrimage walking and praying the rosary. It was winter, and the shrine wasn't exactly near, so from the mother's side it was a big sacrifice. The mother would come everyday in front of the hospital at a specific time to check whether he was alive. She made an agreement with the hospital staff to show him everyday through the window. She would hide behind the trees so he wouldn't see her. The mother and doctors wanted to avoid any hysterical outbursts having been separated from his mother. They thought he might forget his mother with time, if he did not see her. After a few months Nicholas was completely healthy to the surprise of the doctors, but his relationship with his parents was never the same.

Now after many years, in a vision, he saw how his mother was hiding behind the tree, being careful that he did not see her. You can imagine how a two year old boy felt in hospital, sick, surrounded by strangers, without his parents visiting him! Not having seen his mother, his soul 'saw' this as though his family did not love him anymore, that they had abandoned him forever. He concluded that he was not wanted in this world and that no one could love him. Even his parents had abandoned him! His attitude was completely wrong; instead it was the complete opposite of what his parents had actually felt for him.

Returning home Nicholas had forgotten about his stay in hospital. He had suppressed it in his memories, but he was not able suppress the attitude of his soul towards what happened forever. When he had a child himself, his subconscious was once again alert. Not only did the feeling of abandonment return, but his relationship created in that age towards his parents, had completely prevented him from accepting his own child.

The Holy Spirit gave him a vision which helped him understand what actually happened to him, so he was able to forgive his parents and – because he realized what they had truly felt – now he was able to love them again in the correct way. Visiting (after long period of time) his parents after prayer, he was able to hug his mother and tell her that he truly loves her. His relationship towards his son and wife had completely changed. With his son he had an intimate relationship, but unfortunately, his wife is still not prepared to forgive him and accept him back. I believe if whoever reads his testimony and places his wife in their prayers, then God's grace will heal her wounds!

From the moment of our conception things happen to us that we cannot correctly comprehend and therefore we cannot accept them in the correct way. The Bible tells us that only truth can liberate us. Every person yearns for happiness, yearns for blessings, but only a few know what a blessing is. What does it mean to live in blessedness? Is that life in abundance? Life without pain!? Life without fear and sickness!? Is it a blessing to be accepted, loved, valued...? Even if we have all that, it still would not be a blessing the way God would've prepared for His beloved children. We know that life does not exist without disappointment, pain and falls. No one has ever lived such a life, but still many continue to strive for such a life!

I already said that a blessing is the opposite of a curse. The Bible tells us that the people of Israel, because of their sin fell into a curse, which was expressed in a specific way: even though their eyes, their ears and their minds were healthy, they still could not see hear or understand the truth (see Is 6.9-10). Therefore a blessing is the opposite: seeing the world with God's eyes, seeing the world with God's ears and understanding the world with God's heart! All the treasures and wealth of this world and all it's honour and tribute is dirt compared to a soul that can see, hear and understand, with a soul that 'lives' in God! (Cf. CCC 27)

Nicholas' soul had immediately seen, heard and understood. Nicholas wouldn't exchange that moment - when God intervened directly in his soul bringing salvation to an important part of his character - for all the treasures of this world. During prayer Nicholas wasn't only liberated from his wrong attitudes but because of

God's direct 'contact', he was also liberated from the feeling of abandonment and through inner healing and liberation he 'met' God in his soul. We could say that he met a 'part' of God. God was not a stranger to him anymore. The short term spiritual experience left a long term consequence on his being. He experienced what the prophet Isaiah announced a long time ago to everyone who would want God:

> (Is 26.9)
> *"My soul yearns for you in the night, my spirit within me keeps vigil for you."*

His soul was filled with joy and peace, because through the spirit, he had found the truth which his soul was yearning for years!

In baptism God opens the door of our heart, the door to the Kingdom, He acknowledges us as His adopted children, and He enters our heart and calls us to accept Him as our beloved Father. Baptism liberates us from the curse of death caused by original sin, but still the consequences stay: ignorance, the tendency to sin and death, feeling of abandonment by God... (see CCC 403, CCC 405).

God, during baptism, opens the door of His heart by which we can 'enter' through prayer whenever we want to (see CCC 27). Our whole life then can become a prayer; we can live 'hidden' in God! We can freely say that prayer is a method by which we enter God's presence! In God we learn the truth about our life and it brings about change (liberation – salvation) of the soul. But the body and the world draw the soul away from God with all their might. And it is possible to do this because our character is weakened. Then the soul tries to find answers to the questions that arise by the typical logical judgement of this world and sometimes even in occultism, heretical beliefs, esotericism or other flawed solutions. I have to say that all human knowledge and philosophy that really seek the truth - and all monotheistic religions too - do arrive at part of the truth, but the complete truth we can find in the embodied Word – Christ! And there is no need to judge non Christians and see them as less worthy than ourselves, because some of them, although their doctrines seem heretical to us, respect the law of conscience in their hearts, and have become better people then many Christians! We have to testify to the truth with our lives so that they will be drawn to it. It is sad when Christians discard their truth and look for it elsewhere. Many of those Christians, who should have been models for others, have instead turned truth to hypocrisy. They have lost their light-heartedness and have only negative testimonies of faith.

The psalmist tells us that peace can only be found in God. Jesus tells us that He is the only one that can give us peace. Life in God is life in peace. Praying the joyful mysteries, we go through our own lives together with Mary in God. When we pray the rosary with our whole being, we are in fact uniting the mysteries of our own life, (or the lives of those for whom we are praying,) with the mysteries of Jesus' and Mary's life. In that way we find the truth about God, but at the same time about ourselves too. When we unite these mysteries, it brings liberation, and this allows sincere forgiveness of those who hurt us and of ourselves too, it brings remorse for our own flawed judgement or attitudes provoked by inner wounds, or by a sinful relationship with ourselves or another human being who sinned against us. Through forgiveness and repentance we experience inner healing and liberation. This further leads either to physical healing, or a heartfelt 'acceptance' of the sufferings resulting from that relationship. Uniting with the mysteries also produces **firm hope** in eternal life, which will carry us through those situations where healing is inaccessible, and we cannot find meaning to our sufferings. In those situations hope in eternal life is what will give meaning to our life!

Blessing for a soul means only one thing: uniting them with God. A soul that knows God, knows peace!

The personality of our soul is expressed also with emotions. They are created by God and they are good while under control. In specific situations we can feel good or bad, comfortable or uncomfortable; we can be in fear or in peace... Imagine walking on a beam with just one support in the middle. The further we distance ourselves from where the beam begins on the support, it bends more and more under our weight, we are then in danger of slipping off it. Imagine that the beam is at a height of ten meters! This is a rough picture of what our emotions do to our soul. The support is our common sense. It gives us a balance for the emotions, which in certain situations we can or are allowed to surrender. When we distance ourselves too much, when our emotions (which may be positive or negative), become over emphasized, they begin to control our common sense and they become harmful, regardless of whether they were positive while they were in the correct measurement.

Today we can see on television how people love animals to an absurd degree, especially the endangered species and abandoned. Recently I recognised that it turns into a sickness, or an obsession in some people, where they keep even up to a hundred house pets. On television we can see people who are completely naked, demonstrating because 'animals are being abused'. Through their complete nakedness you can see where their need comes from. I still haven't seen naked people demonstrating for children, who are dying of hunger or badly abused. Those people have lost their equilibrium.

Once I was called to pray for a woman who was crippled with cramps. She was refusing to eat. Her husband and son had died within a short period of one another and she had surrendered to grief and disappointment. This situation brought her to that state. Even though it was harrowing, she shouldn't have allowed herself to surrender to the spirit of grief, because she was responsible for her own life, in which she could have done a lot of good things had she not lost the will to live. She had lost her equilibrium.

When we think of people who fall in love, we can recognise that surrender to the emotions. They forget that love is not only an emotion. In many ways they sentence themselves to suffering in advance because most of the time, what they imagine has nothing got to do with reality! They have lost their equilibrium.

Emotional equilibrium is something that we usually lose slowly: it requires a consistent refusal to accept the true nature of the situation in which we find ourselves. In some situations, that step backwards can be momentary (instant) as for example, when faced with immense fear or pain all of a sudden. Over-emphasized emotions are big enemies for a healthy mind, but they also disturb the soul from hearing the impulse of the Holy Spirit. Remember the prophet Elijah in the cave? God's voice told him to step out and stand on the mount before Yahweh. Before Yahweh came, there was a whirlwind that broke rocks and split hills, then there was an earthquake. After the earthquake there was fire and then, in the end, there was a sound of sheer silence (see 1Kgs 19.9-14). God was in the sound of sheer silence. The whirlwind, earthquake and fire are words that can often describe the strength of our emotions. But overly strong emotions are not beneficial to the soul, they only do damage. If we truly wish to hear God's voice, we have to calm our emotions so that they are as quiet as silence, i.e. at least to a state where we have control over them and not let them control us. When we feel that our emotions are going out of control, simply direct them towards God, bringing Him into the situation which 'produced' those emotions. In that way we will manage to maintain our equilibrium.

Mary under the cross is the best example of this behaviour. How much strength she must have needed to be able to 'control' her emotions so that she could be with her son right up to the end! The apostle John was the only apostle who knew how to 'control' the feeling of fear and for that reason he was able to stand under the cross. We know that the ability to control the emotions comes through prayer.

When we were hurt, when we experienced sudden pain or fear, when over a longer period of time feelings of hurt were renewed carrying with them feelings of having been abandoned and the feeling of being useless, we most likely weren't in a state to be able to clearly 'hear' the voice of reason without prayer which would have directed the negative situation towards God. Attitudes that we had formed at that moment most likely are not good for us. In those situations we are in need of inner healing.

During the stay in our mother's womb we are exposed to the influence of our mother's emotions, as well as emotions of all those who are directly tied to us, for example our father, grandfather, grandmother, brother, sister or some other person in the family. A mother's emotional equilibrium will definitely have a positive influence on the formation of the conceived child, while every extreme and unbalanced emotion has negative consequences on the soul of the child.

If the emotions of our soul are the fruit of our spirit when we are in unity with God, those emotions are always positive, no matter how intense. Remember Mary's Magnificat when she says that her spirit exults for joy in God, her Saviour! But unfortunately, sometimes the human spirit falls under the influence of evil spirits and then the soul cannot control the emotions anymore which bring enormous damage to the overall person.

How many Christians are engaged in fortune-telling and other esoteric visions today! When you go to the esoteric fair which is held annually in Zagreb, it is sad to say that you can see a large number of Christians! Once upon a time people would have been stoned for such acts, the Word of God clearly states who does such things is an abomination to the Lord (See. Dt 18.10-12)

Although hypnosis is not recommended to Christians because it is too risky for the human subconscious - scientists have succeeded in going back through the human memory, as far as the moment of conception through it. The hypnotized patient doesn't know how to relate what happened in those moments, but through their emotional reaction it has been easy to conclude what the situation was like at the moment of their conception, and in most situations the parents confirmed it's authenticity.

Not all children were wanted and conceived in marital love. Some people were conceived out of wedlock, in a sinful relation, which had inevitably brought negative emotions. One drastic example is the children who were conceived in the act of rape. We can only imagine the mother's fear and this is reflected on the child's soul.

We can also imagine a mother's fear in a premarital relationship, knowing that her parents condemn such acts and that there would be consequences if she conceives. The matter is even worse if the future mother – due to a lack of education or if she is only a child herself – cannot accept or want the child.

Most children are conceived in marital relations and parents are not even aware that the conception has taken place and therefore do not have a significant emotional reaction. In the mystery of the annunciation we will include the parent's first reactions when they realize they have conceived a child. Undoubtedly the mother's reaction is more important and stronger because the child at that moment is bonded more with the mother than the father. Mother's reactions are sometimes emotionally very strong and the child will not have problems if the reaction was full of enthusiasm and joy, but there will be problems if she was disappointed, fearful, feeling guilty, or hate and feelings where the spirit of the baby clearly picks up the signal that it is not welcome. The influence of those emotions on the formation of characteristics in the soul will depend on the strength and duration of such emotions. Sometimes those people have serious emotional and mental problems, when they themselves conceive a child because the situation awakens their sub consciousness and brings to the surface what was suppressed a long time ago but was never healed.

In most instances the mother in the end accepts and loves her child, but this slowly becomes a suppression of what was earlier felt and it is just a matter of time before the subconscious surfaces in the form of feelings of having been abandoned and in feelings of guilt. We know that unfortunately a large number of conceived children never arrive at birth, because they are aborted - killed. Those children don't only die with a deep feeling of abandonment and unwanted ness but also in great fear. The fear of death is in every human being from the moment of conception. At the moment of conception every human being is gifted with a spirit by God, a created body and soul. Anyone who is even slightly intelligent will 'recognise' the seed of a complete human body in the zygote, even though it is not yet developed to the end. It contains the whole programming for a human body, similar to an acorn which 'hides' a whole oak. But as soon as the acorn falls on fertile soil and sprouts, it is not an acorn anymore but an oak tree!

Sometimes parents, especially mothers, for various reasons, believe that the child should not have been conceived, especially when the conception happens in adultery, premarital relations or during rape. Not all mothers have an equal share of awareness of responsibility, so they don't all react in the same way. Nevertheless, most mothers have a deep feeling of guilt when the conception happened in a way that wasn't 'suitable'. Children conceived in such conditions – once they grow up and enter marital relations – very often suffer from feelings of guilt. Even though sexual relations are a blessing of God for all married couples, those people will probably have a feeling that what they are doing is not right for their whole life. Of course an 'unsuitable' conception is only one of the reasons which can lead to that, but nevertheless it is important to mention and it requires healing!

Very often parents can not 'accept' a newly conceived child for mere materialistic reasons. When a child is conceived in poverty, it is 'normal' for parents to fear that they will not be able to feed one more mouth. Sometimes children are born in families that can feed them without any problem if they forego something which they had planned on. If the fear is intense, the child will most likely suffer from complexes of poverty. Even though some of those children will be well-endowed or rich in life, they will constantly suffer from the complexes that they are spending too much on themselves. They will not have problems when they have to buy something for someone else, but if they were, for example, to buy themselves a normal sandwich they will probably have the feeling of spending too much 'on expensive meat-products'. Those people will often try to 'justify' themselves in front of others when they do buy something new. Most people who could have bought a new car without any difficulty will never do so.

Those, whose parents saw them as a burden because with their conception they were denied a career, or some other plan, can very often suffer from the complex of exploitation which amongst other things can manifest itself as uncontrollable tight-fisted ness.

There are instances where one of the parents, or maybe both, is completely indifferent when a child is conceived, and up to the moment of their birth are not bonded at all to them emotionally. Those children can have a specific complex of identity; it depends on a combination of other circumstances.

It is up to us to consider all the possible circumstances (I was not able to list them all here!) and consider the potential negative consequences. It is necessary not only for us to see the necessity of inner healing, but also with our own testimonies we can help others not to make the same mistakes and be able to accept ourselves as we are: weak and above all in need of God's love. The fact is that we are not all the same, and we do not react the same way in similar circumstances which we might come across in life. Unfortunately, there are people who do not have strong enough defence mechanisms and who have suffered great emotional 'damage' in the first few years of life and this damage doesn't allow them to live believing in God's promises. For that reason, we can never judge anyone because we will never fully know the reasons for someone's 'deviant' behaviour. People are in need of our prayers and never our judgement! We are Christians who through prayer have to represent and fight for our injured brothers, even though - through human eyes - those brothers deserve judgement and not charity. Not one person on this earth deserves our judgement. Sin has to be judged, but not the sinner (see Rom 7.14-25)!

We can make a hypothesis that every person who is momentarily living on this planet is our close relative. Of course, that isn't possible, but when you see a person that through human eyes merits condemnation, imagine that it could have been our Father/Mother, Brother, Sister, Son or Daughter! Would you still condemn them?

One thing is sure: every person is the Son or Daughter of almighty God, our beloved Father. Every person is our Brother or Sister that we don't know well. Can we condemn anyone and then come before God in prayer as though we haven't done anything wrong?

Praying the rosary teaches us how to accept, forgive and love...Praying the first joyful mystery of the rosary, we are united with the conception of Jesus. The joy of his arrival in the world slowly turns into the joy of our arrival in the world. The love with which his parents accepted Him slowly becomes our love. We begin to realize that we came into this world through our parents and but that our true Father is God who adopted us through the death of His only Son on the cross. From the same cross His Son gave us our Mother. Their love will never disappoint us. At a certain point of our lives we will realize that our earthly parents meant a lot, but they too are only children of God, i.e. our Brother and Sister. It is especially important to know this so that when they are in their old age, we will be able to return the love and concern which they had given us in our infancy and childhood.

Through this mystery many can be liberated from the feeling of abandonment, unwanted ness and guilt, which they carry throughout their whole lives. Through this mystery most will learn how to accept their own child when God decides to 'entrust' them with one and through them 'enter' this world.

The Annunciation is also the mystery where we can accept God's will for our life. Firstly accepting that the reason why we are created is that we can inherit salvation (see Jn 17.2-3) and then accept everything that belongs to us as children and successors of Jesus. Primarily I am speaking about the enormous grace which God wishes to give us already in this life, that is-unification with Himself. This grace carries with it a responsibility with regard to life and with regard to the lives of our brothers and sisters to the extent that God would expect of us. We can identify ourselves with such a range of figures – from the apostle John to the apostle Paul, or from St. Teresa, the little flower to Padre Pio. ... Will God give us that grace to be able to love Him, and will he simply 'bask' in our love and not expect anything else except to love Him, or will He give us the grace to evangelize, to be a reaper of souls for Him - it is up to Him to decide. Every grace that God wishes to give us, we have to humbly accept, regardless of our capabilities or wishes. God through His gifts does what is best for us, and we are there to support Him with our own free will and effort.

Therefore in the first joyful mystery of the rosary we receive:

- ◆ Acceptance and meaning for our personal life and lives of those whom we are praying for;
- ◆ Healing of the negative influences at the moment of conception and up to the moment that the parents found out about it, also liberation from the feeling of abandonment, being unwanted, feeling of guilt, unworthiness, beginning from the moment of and after conception;
- ◆ Liberation from the fear of death, which is the root of many other fears;
- ◆ Accepting God's gifts correctly regardless of how big they are in our eyes;
- ◆ Accepting God as a good Father, accepting our adoption, by which we have to live in this world

instead of Jesus and continue His work where he left off in the manner that our Father wants it;

♦ Accepting fellow human beings as brothers and sisters;

♦ Accepting the Holy Spirit as a divine person who comes to us so that we will have life to the fullest;

♦ Accepting God's closeness as the biggest blessing that we can strive for;

♦ Accepting God's help in many different ways also through the direct influence of our guardian angel in our lives;

♦ Accepting everything that the Holy Spirit will 'reveal' to us in further 'meditation' of the mystery of Jesus' conception, so that we can be a blessing to ourselves and to others for whom we are praying!

The second joyful mystery
– Mary carried Jesus to visit Elizabeth

See the extract from Luke's gospel!

(Lk 1.39-56)
*"In those days Mary set out and went with haste
to a Judean town in the hill country, where she
entered the house of Zechariah and greeted Elizabeth. When Elizabeth heard Mary's greeting,
the child leapt in her womb. And Elizabeth was
filled with the Holy Spirit, exclaimed with a loud
cry, 'Blessed are you among women, and blessed
is the fruit of your womb. And why has this happen to me, that the mother of my Lord comes
to me? For as soon as I heard the sound of your
greeting, the child in my womb leapt for joy. And
blessed is she who believed that there would be a
fulfilment of what was spoken to her by the Lord."*

The Canticle of Mary
*"Mary said: 'My soul magnifies the Lord, and
my spirit rejoices in God my Saviour for he was
looked on the lowliness of his servant. Surely,
from now on all generations will call me blessed;
for the Mighty One has done great things for me,*

and holy is his name. His mercy is for those who fear him from generation to generation.

He has shown strength with his arm, he has scattered the proud in the thoughts of their hearts. He has brought down the powerful from their thrones, and lifted up the lowly.

he has filled the hungry with good things, and sent the rich away empty.

He has helped his servant Israel, in remembrance of his mercy, according to the promise he made to our ancestors, to Abraham and to his descendants forever.'

And Mary remained with her for about three months and then returned to her home."

Let's analyse the text!

Mary had set out towards Elizabeth, who lived in the hill country in the town of Judah. The evangelist emphasizes that Mary had hastily set out towards Elizabeth, which does not mean that she moved at great speed, but rather that she had hastily set out after she had found out that Elizabeth was pregnant. We can also conclude that the conception of Jesus took place quite soon after the annunciation. The 'hastily' can also uncover the reason of her visit to Elizabeth. Some believe that Mary went to Elizabeth so that people would not notice that she is in a 'blessed state', also not to disgrace herself or Joseph. This is not logical because in the first days, pregnancy cannot be noticed, but if she had truly wanted to hide her pregnancy, she would not have returned from Elizabeth after three months, because it would then be possible to notice the fact that she was with child.

Others believe that Elizabeth needed Mary's help. Elizabeth was the wife of a well-known priest and it is likely that she had plenty of servants to take care of her. Mary's visit was for *spiritual* reasons. The angel, who announced to Mary that Elizabeth conceived, didn't say that Elizabeth needed help. Rather he said that God had powerfully intervened in her life through this miraculous conception. Mary had firstly wanted to share her experience with Elizabeth. Elizabeth was one of those rare people who would have been able to understand Mary, precisely because of her own experience. Whoever receives a great grace from God, would want to share that experience with someone who would understand him or her. I imagine that we'd agree on the fact that the two of them must have spent time together in conversation, prayer, canticles and mutual support.

Finally, the Holy Spirit was the One who wanted Mary to hear Elizabeth's words of support, spoken by Him; the Holy Spirit was the one that wanted through Mary to say the canticle of the 'Magnificat', which will be sung to the end of the world! The spiritual environment, in which Mary spent the first three months of her pregnancy, was a necessary requisite for her to be able to 'bear' everything that awaited her in the months ahead, and also – dare I say – her whole life! It was also important for Jesus in the first three critical months in Mary's womb to be protected from the negative environment of this world.

The meeting of the two mothers took place in Zechariah's house, where Mary first greeted Elizabeth. As soon as Elizabeth heard Mary's greeting, the first thing she felt was her baby leaping for joy and then she was filled with the Holy Spirit. We mentioned earlier that the Holy Spirit can fill certain people or the power of the Holy Spirit comes upon them enabling them to carry out specific tasks or services, or gives them specific graces. In this case the Holy Spirit opened the eyes of Elizabeth's heart so that she could see the spiritual reality, which in other ways would be completely impossible to visualize. Therefore we can consider Elizabeth's words as the direct words of the Holy Spirit. Elizabeth's words were a prophecy, i.e. God had spoken through her!

Elizabeth then, filled with the Holy Spirit, loudly blessed Mary. She also prophesized a great truth; that Mary is the most blessed of all women ever born! Earlier in this book I said that the biggest blessing is the enjoyment of being adopted by God and the friendship of a direct relationship with Him. Mary not only enjoyed being a child of God and His friendship, but she was also able to enjoy the Motherhood of God! No other woman was ever, or will ever be, that close to

God the way she was, and she still is and always will be – Mary. Mary was the one who was able to love without any limits, because that love was embedded in her twice: firstly in a sinless conception, where she was protected from the shame of original sin and secondly when she was fulfilled with the Holy Spirit in the moment that she conceived the God-man in her womb. Mary had given God love in the way God had foreseen it for all of us. Elizabeth's blessing not only contained Mary's life of this world with Jesus, but she also in her spirit saw millions of souls to whom Mary would become a mother. She saw those for whom Mary would be a consolation, a hope, a joy and a sure road to her Son. I know that I am one of them! For that reason, I bless you Mary!

Elizabeth then blesses Jesus, i.e. the fruit of Mary's womb. Elizabeth 'straight away' mentions that Mary is in a blessed state. Seeing that Elizabeth said those words as soon as Mary greeted her, it could not be the fruit of an earlier conversation (because it never took place), or the fruits of any former information. Those words would have meant a lot to Mary as support for the decision she had made. We have to bear in mind that Mary was aware of her relationship with Joseph the whole time and that she would have to face him! Elizabeth's words were words of support, but they were also a confirmation from God with regard to what had happened. We can be sure that Mary was not spared trials and that the devil was fighting to prevent the birth of

Jesus with all his strength. Trials and contrariety are often proof that what we began with God's inspiration was truly from God. God always gives us consolation in moments of trial, only if we know how to recognize them and accept them in the right way.

We can ask ourselves why the Holy Spirit said that Mary is the most blessed among women through the mouth of Elizabeth and that Jesus is blessed? Some might even think that Mary received a bigger honour than Jesus. Many people throughout the centuries argued that those who prayed to Mary gave her greater honour then God Himself. We know that that isn't true. Elizabeth said that Mary is 'blessed amongst women'. Some could say that there were women who were blessed in the same way or even more blessed – which in the spiritual sense is impossible. If a blessing means intimacy and the closeness of God, then we can be completely sure that Mary was the most blessed. If Elizabeth had said 'most blessed is the fruit in your womb', instead of 'blessed is the fruit in your womb', there most likely would be some who would interpret this as a proof that Mary had more 'fruit in her womb', i.e. more children among whom Jesus was the most blessed. For this reason the Holy Spirit clearly states that Mary was a virgin throughout her whole life because Elizabeth's words cannot be linked with some other future pregnancies because she didn't use the prefix 'most'.

The more we honour Mary in our heart, the more we honour God, who created man and gave man the same intimacy that He gave to Mary. Mary in this sense is like a fore-taste of heaven for anyone who can understand this correctly. Looking at everything that God had given Mary and what she gave back to Him in return, we can better understand what kind of relationship we will have with Him one day when we live close to Him for the whole of eternity.

Elizabeth filled with the Holy Spirit prophesied (God spoke through her) that Mary became the Mother of our Lord. We know that Elizabeth's Lord – is God. Without doubt God has pronounced Mary His mother. Throughout the centuries, worshippers will call Mary the 'Mother of God' and quite rightly too.

We also have to know too though that Mary isn't the *creator* of God, but simply – his Mother. God had always wanted to come amongst us - but in the same way as we came: He wanted to be born of woman. For someone to be born, he or she needs a mother. Mary had received the exceptional honour to be the one through whom God came to live amongst us in a body. All of us were in God's plan before conception. So we can say we existed – in God's plan – even before we were conceived. As I already mentioned, we actually enter this world through our parents and God entrusts them to care for our upbringing.

In that way we can understand that we truly belong to God and not to our parents. We were only a 'gift' and 'entrusted' so that through them we enter the world and for them to take care of us until we become independent enough to be able to take care for ourselves and for us to worry about them when they are prepared to leave this world. Through our parents we enter this world, as their children we are responsible to care and pray for them and 'see them off' into eternity.

Mary is the Mother through whom God wanted to come in a visible way amongst us and God entrusted to her the care of His own self. This care was not only material – but even more so, spiritual. The devil must have wanted with all his power to destroy the life of Jesus, and Mary was the one who gave Him the best protection spiritually. We sometimes read in the Gospel that Jesus spent almost all of His free time in personal prayer. We know that He did that because praying was necessary for life. For Jesus, one fountain of strength was found in prayer. But when he couldn't pray, prayers were still necessary for him the same way. We know that Mary together with her husband Joseph prayed for Jesus, not only in His childhood but right up to His death on the cross. Only when we enter eternity we will realize how important Mary's prayers were in the life of Jesus. It was the most important part of the life which Mary had given Him. It is also what we need of our parents, but what parent understands this? For that reason Jesus offers us His Mother from the Cross so that she is a Mother to us – only if we wish her to be, i.e. if we want to become her children? Truly, if we want Mary to become our Mother, we must first become her children of our own free will!

God also wanted to have a Mother so that He could receive love from someone because up till then no one was able to love God in a way He had always longed for. How much love and gentleness did God receive from Mary and she never ever asked for anything in return! Just think though – when our parents pass away – we do not stop referring to them as our parents, so too with Jesus: God throughout eternity cannot stop referring to Mary as His Mother. Just like us – after our child dies – we don't stop being a loving Father and Mother to her or him; so too with Mary after Jesus' death she did not stop being a Mother. If, for some reason, Jesus would have broken the mother-son relationship with Mary – what could we hope for? Wouldn't God then break with us the son-ship relationship, would we not cease to be children of God? Of course that is not possible because God in His essence is Love. For these reasons, Mary is the Mother of my Lord!

Elizabeth had then affirmed that Mary's greeting made the baby leap for joy in her womb. This sentence is important to us because it treats of a number of facts. John the Baptist who was then in his sixth month of life after conception, was able to spiritually recognize Jesus who was only in His first month since conception. Of course the Holy Spirit had given him that knowledge! For us it is important that Jesus in his first days after conception was not only a foetus but rather He was Jesus, and He was Elizabeth's Lord. The Holy Spirit had called the 'foetus' not even thirty days old our *Lord* (and I daresay he was probably only a few days old), and Mary His mother! Therefore we know that John the Baptist was filled with the Holy Spirit while still in his mother's womb (see Lk 1.15). For us it is important to recognize too that John's spirit had reacted using John's whole body. His spirit was filled with joy and the body showed its joy by leaping in his Mother's womb.

Along the way we will notice there really exists a time and place for everything and also for showing joy, but when the Holy Spirit overpowers someone, very often that person cannot even 'control' it - even in the womb, let alone in the Church. For some people today, it is disturbing when people are joyful or dancing or clapping their hands when they meet Jesus, but here we have an example how John the Baptist even before birth could not hold back his joy of meeting our Lord. I personally believe that we are all different and should take into consideration that different people show their joy in different ways and that joy is always spontaneous if it is sincere. Even though I experience my joy in a deep peace, a feeling that I belong to God, I am still really happy when I see young people show their joy and enthusiasm when they meet the living God: even if they do it through song, dance, clapping, crying or other 'unusual expressions'. I am joyful when I see people joyful because of the Lord. Today it is so rare that it would be really senseless to silence someone who is truly joyful in our Lord. I believe it is more meaningless to participate in liturgy with a cold heart, without any expression of your being or without any emotions, than let's say rejoicing even though for some it is inappropriate. It reminds me of David and his daughter Michal (see 1 Chr 15).

Our spirit 'sees' what is happening around us from the moment of our conception. If we are immersed in our Father's and Mother's prayers, we are immersed in the Holy Spirit. Our parent's prayers can 'carry' us to God's closeness where we will have protection from wrong conclusions and from over emphasized emotions. I have very often watched small children newly born and most of them can 'see' better than adults in faith: They are in a position to recognize danger where their parents don't even notice it. Take this example that is indicative: If a child was conceived in a Christian marriage and regularly prayed for, and you were to put a picture of Sai Baba or some other false prophet above the bed where they sleep, there are reactions of fear and restlessness. Often there are nightmares too. Most parents don't know that Sai Baba is a false prophet and a servant of the evil one, but their babies notice it straight away. Why? For this reason – adults, as opposed to babies, communicate with their surroundings by the use of reason – small children communicate through the spirit, which when contrasted with reason is more capable of 'seeing'. The baby doesn't see *a gentle grandad-like figure who talks about love* - a baby very clearly see a horrifying servant of the devil, which

Sai Baba is. Didn't Jesus Himself tell us we should be like small children?

For the ancient Jews it was customary for a mother to hide her pregnancy as long as possible, at least for the first six months. The reason for this was so that the child could be protected as long as possible from negative surroundings which were considered most dangerous for the child's soul. We all know that our first impressions are often the most distinct and the most determining. Immersing ourselves in this mystery, it can bring us inner healing and liberation from the negative influences that we received as unborn babies and much more, and at the same time we acknowledge our personal weakness and our need for God.

Through Elizabeth, the Holy Spirit then blessed Mary, because she believed what was announced to her by our Lord. We must draw attention here to the fact that Elizabeth uses the same word: "Lord" when she speaks about Mary as the *Mother of our Lord* and when she talks about *Who* spoke to Mary through the angel. Through Elizabeth, the Holy Spirit blesses Mary because she believed. Praying the rosary we can be sure that we will gain the necessary strength of faith to accept whatever task God wishes to entrust to us by entering *this* mystery. At the same time we become more open to possible inspirations of the Holy Spirit, and therefore more capable of recognizing and accepting them.

Under the influence of Elizabeth's words, Mary lifts up her spirit and sings her canticle, which was to become the most well-known and most sung canticle of Christians throughout the ages. What Mary had said in her canticle, could not have come just from her mind. She was inspired by the Holy Spirit, who had prophesized through her in that way.

Mary in the canticle speaks about her inner experience of God in that situation. She speaks of her soul and her spirit reacting to everything that had happened to her. Her soul glorifies the Lord and her spirit rejoices. It is one of the few places in the Bible where God tells us that the inner person consists of a spirit and a soul. It is important to notice that Mary says that her *spirit rejoices in God her Saviour*. Her spirit was with God at that moment. We can say that it was closely tied with God's spirit. In fact, that is the main task of our spirit: to be in direct connection with God. Every prayer has to abide in God, more concretely in the Holy Spirit, through our spirit. The spirit is the part of us that has the ability to 'enter' God's presence and in that way bond our soul with God. A bonded soul is illuminated with God's truth. It is liberated from wrong attitudes and understandings which we created by trying to understand what was happening to us and to others around us without the illumination of the Holy Spirit. When we enter God's presence with our spirit, our soul experiences inner illumination and healing, therefore we become open to the Holy Spirit to work through His various gifts and charismas.

Mary's celebration and rejoicing was caused by God's act of mercifully looking at a servant, who, in the eyes of the world was an unknown person and He then gifted the world with the long awaited Saviour. God had compassion on an unknown girl and He sent his Son to the world as a Saviour. Mary was not saved by the death of Jesus on the cross because she was born without original sin and conceived as a child of God, but her salvation consisted in Jesus' saving her, 'barring' her from the shame of original sin; not allowing it to invade her before conception. Metaphorically speaking, someone can save us by pulling us out of a pit that we could never have come out of by ourselves, or he could save us by preventing us from falling into the pit in the first place. At the moment we become children of God, He pulls us out of the world of darkness, i.e. from the pit and in that way saves us, but that salvation is not finished. It continues throughout our whole life. God further saves us from falling into the pit from which He pulled us. Unfortunately many have returned to the pit from which they came. We have to realize that often we don't 'see' the good paths and we need our Saviour who will save us from falling in again. Therefore Jesus Christ is the Saviour who pulls us out from the power of death, but the Holy Spirit is our personal Saviour who saves us from 'falling' back into the pit! A soul wounded by original sin desires to sin and is in need of healing; he or she is in need of a complete transformation, so that they endure the road to salvation. For that reason, God gives us His mystical body – the Church. In unity with the Church we can find everything that God has prepared for us so that we can inherit eternal life.

Mary further says: "From this day on, all generations will call me 'blessed'. Because the almighty has done great things for me, holy is his name. He has mercy on those who fear him in every generation."

We can discern here that Mary's spirit 'sees' the future, right up to the end of time. The Holy Spirit *let* her understand that all generations, till the end of time, would call her blessed, so that her joy would be greater. To be blessed means to be bonded with God. We can see that *that* was God's intention and wish: for us to call Mary blessed. The statement gave Mary joy in the Holy Spirit. In a different context, it would be misleading to call her blessed. The reason for her being called blessed - and it was the Holy Spirit who first called her that - was that God had done incredibly powerful things in her and she had returned it with pure love. This is a God whose mercy never ends towards people who truly honour Him.

Connection with the mystery

What does this mystery remind us of? Of our own lives, from the moment of conception to the moment of birth! We will unite this mystery with the moments spent in our mother's womb before birth. Mothers and

Fathers carry large responsibilities for their children. The moments of formation in the mother's womb are especially important. In this mystery, we examine the mission we received from God and our relation towards what God gave us.

I already mentioned that a child in its mother's womb 'communicates' with its surroundings. The spirit of the baby is aware of what is happening around him, but if he or she is not 'immersed' in the parent's prayers, the soul hasn't the light of the Holy Spirit to be able to correctly accept what is happening around him and with him, so he or she cannot develop correct relationships towards the people with whom their lives are linked and towards the surroundings they are exposed to. Children in their mother's womb can be exposed to a number of negative influences for example:

♦ Abandonment by one or both parents,

♦ Fear of death because either the mother was thinking of aborting, or maybe had an unsuccessful attempt at aborting,

♦ Fear of a mother's or father's bond with occultism,

♦ - Unwanted ness by other members of the family, for example, a grandfather or grandmother, brother or sister,

♦ Feelings of guilt or unworthiness because of parents constant fighting,

- Exposure to occultism through fortune telling, amulets for protection or witchcraft,

- Imprecation of evil on the child by parents, or people whether close or distant while still in the mother's womb,

- A mother's or father's misunderstanding of God or maybe even involvement in heresy or idolatry,

- A mother's fear of losing the baby due to sickness, or due to the experience of previous miscarriages, which might as adults turn into a fear of losing loved ones or push adults into an unreasonable state of jealousy,

- Psychological or physical sickness of the mother, which can negatively affect the baby,

- Drugs or other mother's addictions, which can also have negative affects on the baby,

- Inherited consequences of curses (see Dt 27 and 28; Is 6. 9-10)

- Many other consequences which can be revealed to us through prayer in the Holy Spirit.

The second mystery 'unites' us with the time of Jesus' stay in Mary's womb. Participating spiritually in the mystery, we and those for whom we are praying, will slowly experience inner healing and liberation, which can very positively be seen in everyday life. Many of the wrong attitudes that we have and many mental and physical disorders can be associated with the period of stay in our mother's womb. Many people drastically change their personality and are liberated of the attachments and the bonds they have on people, things and surroundings through praying this mystery. In it they receive healing and liberation.

During prayer it maybe be possible to 'feel' what we felt in our mother's womb, so people praying this mystery in spirit feel great pain, loneliness, abandonment and fear. But in prayer, these feelings do not affect the person praying negatively, nor the person that they are praying for. Instead they bring joy because they liberate and heal. It is similar to the joy that people feel when they unite their suffering with Christ's through the special charisma for suffering. During prayer we do not have to 'participate' with our soul and body in what our spirit is experiencing, but simply let it continue and pass over us as though it doesn't concern us. It is possible through the actual gift of that prayer.

In the second joyful mystery, we pray for our own personal call which we received from God, whether it is a calling to become a priest, nun, evangelizer or parent, whether it is to build a church, or any other inspiration which we can with appropriate proof, know that it is coming from God. Every call which comes from God brings great difficulties with it and requires supernatural faith on our part. Uniting our call or mission in the second joyful mystery with Mary's mission, we will receive light and strength from the Holy Spirit to endure and to achieve what God intended for us. This mystery is intended for every labourer in God's field, no matter where it is and what God's intention for it is. If we succeed in *opening* our spirit to be able to accept as much as God wishes to give, then many of God's *labourers* through our prayer of the rosary will receive the strength and endurance to go on. They will always be renewed in the strength of the Holy Spirit to practice their mission in the best way possible. Many amongst them, who begin to doubt in their career or mission, can find support once again or will experience a boost in their faith through our prayer, which will allow them to persevere and to *labour on*!

When we enter into this mystery, we will be united with many 'Elizabeths', who will become true brothers and sisters and with whom we can share our joy and faith, but also our trials and needs. This mystery in a special way opens our spirit to be able to carry out the mission that we are striving to live. Love and thankfulness to God will grow in our hearts as we begin to comprehend our lives as a gift from a Father who loves us immensely.

This mystery gives us the strength to accept life the way it is: with all its trials and sufferings and with all the joyful days that we experience too.

The third joyful mystery
– **The birth of Jesus**

Let's take a look at what the Gospel says:

(Lk 2.1-20)
"In those days a decree went out from Emperor Augustus that all the world should be registered. This was the first registration, and was taken while Quirinius was governor of Syria. All went to their own towns to be registered. Joseph also went from the town of Nazareth in Galilee to Judea, to the city of David called Bethlehem, because he was descended from the house and family of David. He went to be registered with Mary, to whom he was engaged, and who was expecting a child. While they were there, the time came for her to deliver her child. And she gave birth to her firstborn son and wrapped him in bands of cloth and laid him in a manger, because there was no place for them in the inn.

The Shepherds and the Angels

In that region there were shepherds living in the fields keeping watch over their flock by night. Then an angel of the Lord stood before them and the glory of the Lord shone around them, and they were terrified. Then the angel said to them,

"Do not be afraid; for see - I am bringing you good news of great joy for all the people: For today in the city of David a saviour has been born for you who is Messiah, the Lord. And this will be a sign for you: you will find a child wrapped in bands of cloth and lying in a manger."

And suddenly there was with the angel a multitude of the heavenly host praising God and saying: 'Glory to God in the highest heaven and on earth peace among those whom He favours!'

When the angels had left them and gone to heaven, the shepherds said to one another, "Let us go, now, to Bethlehem to see this thing that has taken place, which the Lord has made known to us." So they went with haste and found Mary and Joseph, and the child lying in the manger. When they saw this, they made known what had been told them about this child and all who heard it were amazed at what the shepherds told them. But Mary treasured all these words, and pondered them in her heart. The shepherds returned, glorifying and praising God for all they had heard and seen, as it had been told them."

Let's analyse the text!

Today we know - it can be scientifically proven - that the person Jesus truly existed. Few historical people have left more evidence of their existence the way Jesus Christ did, and yet many doubt that He ever existed. Here I won't list all the evidence. To the sceptical, I simply want to say that if you want proof of the authenticity of Jesus' life, use the same criterion you would use for any other historical person (e.g. Socrates, Plato...), and you will be surprised at how many proofs there are. Therefore, Jesus was born in Judea, in the town of Bethlehem. Although most of His life he lived in the Galilean town of Nazareth which is why they called Him the Nazarene. He was born at the time when Quirinius was governor of Syria and it was the same year that the decree went out from Caesar Augustus that the whole world should be enrolled. Every Israelite had to enrol at the place from which they came. So did Joseph. Since he was from David's descent, he went to the town of Bethlehem. It happened at the time that Mary was due to give birth.

According to the Old Testament, the Messiah had to be a descendent of David and be born in David's town of Bethlehem. The circumstances of His birth were peculiar. So why didn't God smooth everything out so that Joseph would be a resident of Bethlehem. Then everyone would know that the Messiah was from Bethlehem? We must bear in mind that Herod issued a command that all male children up to the age of two be killed. Even though Jesus escaped death because the angel warned Joseph in his dream to move his family to Egypt, imagine what could have happened if after Herod's death they returned back to Bethlehem instead of Nazareth? The whole of Bethlehem knew that Herod's army was looking for the newly born Messiah which is why they were killing their children to be sure that they had removed Him forever. But the residents of Bethlehem knew who they were looking for and they knew that they had fled. How could they have known? Well Bethlehem wasn't a large town and the arrival of three wise men from the east, on camels and with escorts, together with the presentation of these gifts to Jesus, meant that they could not have gone unnoticed. Testimonies of the shepherds whom the angels had led to Jesus also revealed who Herod was looking for. We can only imagine how many innocent children were killed and because of that, how much hatred there was towards the Holy Family. For some readers of the Gospel today, it is difficult to understand how Jesus could run away and leave so many innocent children to be killed because of Him. Since the creation of Adam and Eve, many just souls waited in limbo for the Messiah, who was to free them so that they could enter heaven. Who could have told them about the birth of the Messiah, if not the souls of pure children? The tremendous joy they experienced made their pain seem little because they were able to be the first to announce immanent salvation to many holy men and women from Adam to now. We can see that God used Caesar Augustus so that His plan for the birth of the Messiah is completely fulfilled with innocent children to announce the news in limbo!

There was no room in the inn for Jesus' family so they settled themselves in a stable. Stables in those days were on the outside of villages. The only-begotten Son of God was born in dire poverty and separated from people. For us they seem 'inhumane' conditions. It took place during winter when the days, and especially the nights were cold. Was everything that dark? What did Jesus gain by refusing to be born in a luxurious room at the inn or in some palace – He could have been born in much better conditions? Firstly, He received love from poor people in the world. Secondly, he avoided the crowds and noise in Bethlehem caused by the crowds who had come to fill in the register as was commanded. Thirdly, he received the chance to be born in intimacy with His parents, surrounded with love and the prayers of His Mother and Father. The shepherds were able to come and bow to Him without any interference. God wanted *them* to bow to Him first, because they had sincerely waited for Him with love, unlike those who would have seen a 'chance' to profit by the situation like hypocrites. His first moments outside his mother's womb were spent surrounded by people who had sincerely longed for Him and loved Him. He was spared the presence of negative people. Sometimes its worth paying a high price, to ensure that the circumstances are as they should be!

The angel first announced the news of Jesus' birth to the shepherds who took their herds to graze near Bethlehem. The angel clearly calls Jesus the Saviour, the Christ and the Lord. This is exactly the order how we should accept Him in our life. All of a sudden an army of other angels joined this angel who praised God above and called peace upon people because God loves them. Already there we can see how the angel clearly says that the Father had sent His Son because He loves people! He had sent him to bring peace to human hearts. The evangelist Luke tells us that the shepherds found Jesus and that they bowed to Him. I am sure that they didn't bow to the King without any gifts because even then in those days it was unthinkable. I believe that the Holy Family received enough food, necessary for the first days of Jesus' life. Providence had seen to it that He received enough from the poor.

The shepherds described the appearance of the angels and what they said to Mary and Joseph. They listened to these tidings with joy. The words of the Shepherds strengthened their faith. But the shepherds had also talked about the experience to other people and everyone who heard was amazed. We can assume that the same day almost everyone in the region had heard about what had happened.

Mary had cherished all those events in her heart and was thinking about them. That is the main purpose of the Charismatic rosary of intercession: to keep the mysteries of the rosary in our heart and often meditate over them! In that way we open ourselves to the Holy Spirit to work and He will change our whole being so that we can be similar to Christ!

After the shepherds had paid homage to the Child, they returned glorifying God, not only for what happened to the Holy Family and the world in general, but also to themselves. They praised and glorified God because they were the ones who were able to see and hear the angel and were amongst the first to bow to the newborn Messiah. I deeply believe that the shepherds were amongst the rare ones who did not condemn Jesus after the slaughter of innocent children.

The Holy Family, soon after the birth of Jesus, found accommodation at the inn. We read how the wise men from the east found Jesus in a house (see Mt 2:11). They bowed to Him and offered gifts of gold, frankincense and myrrh. These were symbols that they recognized the royal, priestly and prophetic authorities of Jesus. Let's remember here that all of us through baptism receive the same gifts directly from God. Through baptism we become children of God and we all receive the same honours as Jesus, i.e. a royal, priestly and prophetical calling. If only we were able to believe what the Bible and Church teaches us! If only we could accept this gift!

There are four facts from Sacred Scripture that we Christians have difficulty accepting. They are that:

◆ Sacred Scripture tells us about God's love towards us,

◆ Sacred Scripture tells us that we are children of God,

♦ Sacred Scripture tells us what God had done and what He can still do and wants to do for us,

♦ Sacred Scripture talks about what we, as children of God, can do for ourselves and for those around us by the power of the Holy Spirit, which we – as adopted children of our Father – receive in our inheritance and of which we have a preliminary experience in prayer.

Connection with the mysteries

Praying the third joyful mystery we bring the moment of our birth (and the birth of those for whom we are praying), into the mystery of the birth of Jesus Christ. Not just the act of birth but also, its circumstances immediately before and after the birth. Meditating on the circumstances of Jesus' birth, we can easily discern God's perfect love which He offers to each one of us. But what were the circumstances like at the moment of our birth? A lot of people were born in anxiety and faithlessness, in a situation where the parents didn't pray. Those souls could be in fear and pain, in noise and unrest, unwanted and unaccepted, like in many other negative situations. For every child, when it is born, the mental state of the parents is important, especially the mental state of the mother. Are the parents ready to accept the baby eagerly or is his or her birth a burden to them. Do they experience him as a burden, unable to 'accept' him/her as a gift of God?

Praying this mystery we can expect healing and liberation through the intercession of our heavenly mother for a mother's fear before and during the birth. Some mothers bear children with enormous difficulty. This causes fear in the mother both for her own and for her child's life. Sometimes the fear is so strong that it leaves a deep mark on the soul of the newly born baby and that new person suppresses it for the rest of his life. That is especially difficult for future mothers for whom – when they give birth to the baby – suppressed fear could 'awake' in the subconscious and even lead to grave mental problems.

Fear of death in the child caused by a difficult birth is even stronger if the Mother at the beginning of the pregnancy tried to abort. This is because the child associates the leaving of the mother's womb with death.

Deep mental and physical wounds are received through difficult births due to the sickness of the mother or the baby, maybe even due to the incorrect position of the baby in the womb and due to inadequate medical equipment during birth and because of other negative influences.

Mental wounds can be caused by open non-acceptance from one or both parents sometimes it is because the newly born was not the desired gender, or if the child is very sick, or if he/she is an unexpected twin, or born out of wedlock. I have prayed for many women whose fathers for a long time were not able to accept them because they were born as female and not as a male. Often these people through life suffer from various mental inabilities.

Sometimes, those who assist at birth are guilty of murder over and over again if they participated in murder, i.e. abortion. Those people are 'marked' with the spirit of death, which the baby's spirit 'recognizes'. Therefore uniting with this mystery liberates them from negative consequences received this way. It heals them from not accepting the surrounding, i.e. people with whom the family is living.

This mystery encourages us also to accept:
- ♦ Our own gender and appearance,
- ♦ Our parents, the way they are, with all their faults and limitations, also to forgive them for every lack of love and gentleness from conception to birth,
- ♦ Our life as God's gift and the realisation that God rejoices because he created us and for that reason and wants only the very best for us,
- ♦ Everything that the Holy Spirit through Mary's intercession further reveals to us while meditating over this mystery.

Uniting with this mystery we can more easily accept our life the way it actually is. In that way, we can better 'accept' our weaknesses, our sinfulness and imperfections in general. We become aware of the 'imperfections' of people around us. We do not judge them anymore, but instead with our experience strive to bring them close to God, who is the only one that can give them their purpose in life.

It is an established truth that through the mysteries of the rosary we accept ourselves the way we are, which opens our heart so we can accept other people in their imperfections. We begin to realize that every person deserves our love but that every evil requires our judgement too.

The fourth joyful mystery
– Presenting Jesus in the Temple

What actually happened? Let us see!

> (Lk 2:22-38)
> *"When the time came for their purification according to the law of Moses, they brought him up to Jerusalem to present him to the Lord, (as it is written in the law of the Lord: 'Every first-born male shall be designated as holy to the Lord'), and they offered a sacrifice according to what is stated in the law of the Lord 'a pair of turtledoves or two young pigeons,'*
>
> *Now there was a man in Jerusalem whose name was Simeon; this man was righteous and devout, looking forward to the consolation of Israel, and the Holy Spirit rested on him. It had been revealed to him by the Holy Spirit that he would not see death before he had seen the Lord's Messiah. Guided by the spirit, Simeon came into the temple; and when the parents brought in the child Jesus to do for him what is customary under the law, Simeon took him in his arms and praised God, saying:*
>
> *"Master, now you are dismissing your servant in peace, according to your word, for my eyes have*

seen your salvation, which you have prepared in the presence of all peoples, a light for revelation to the Gentiles, and for glory to your people Israel.'

And the child's father and mother were amazed at what was being said about him. Then Simeon blessed them and said to his mother Mary, "This child is destined for the falling and the rising of many in Israel, and to be a sign that will be opposed so that the inner thoughts of many may be revealed - and a sword will pierce your own soul too".

There was also a prophet, Anna, the daughter of Phanuel, of the tribe of Asher. She was of a great age, having lived with her husband seven years after her marriage, and then as a widow to the age of eighty-four. She never left the temple, but worshiped there with fasting and prayer night and day. At that moment she came, and began to praise God, and to speak about the child to all who were looking for the redemption of Jerusalem.

Let's analyse Luke's text!

Eight days after the birth of Jesus, he was circumcised and officially received the name Jesus (originally: Joshua=God saves). Forty days after His birth His parents presented Him in the temple. It happened in Jerusalem, after the forty-day waiting period had passed before Mary's purification (in those times women were considered unclean for forty days after the birth). The main part of the presentation was to make a sacrifice of a burnt offering and a sacrifice for the expiation of sin. By the law, Jesus −as a first born male child − had to be presented to God. What did the presentation represent? Many Jews didn't understand the idea of what God wanted by ordering that the first born should be presented to Him. In Israel the main descendant of the parents was the first born male. This was God's rule. God had wanted to be present in each link of the family lineage in that way. In the presentation, which in fact is an 'abandonment', parents would ask and receive special graces in their family from God through that child. No other child in the family had the right to that sort of blessing. The first born son had the responsibility of carrying on the Jewish faith and tradition of his parents, and to do that, he needed special grace from God. The parents by the act of presentation had put their faith in God's hands so that God could work in a special way in the life of their first born son. By doing that, the continuity of orthodoxy would be preserved and true devotion to God would continue and all family blessings would flow on to the following generation. It was a special expression of God's love towards the chosen people. The first born son, after the death of his parents, would be responsible for his brothers and sisters. He possessed authority which was God given to protect their lives. For that reason he was the source of special blessings for his family, because God, to whom he was presented, was with him and guaranteed the extension of family blessings on further generations. In Israel at that time, most people were only interested in worldly blessings and didn't show interest in spiritual blessings.

Mary and Joseph presented their Son so that God would, in and through that act, lead them in a special way to the actualization of what He foresaw. They weren't interested in wealth, nor power, nor honour, nor strength, but only in achieving the greatest good that man can possess in this world; communion with God. They presented their Son to God so that God's presence would follow Him throughout His whole life.

Carrying a tiny infant to be baptised, we in fact are 'presenting' him/her to God. Through baptism we all become children of God and through our personal decision we become the Father's sons and daughters. At the same time it is not important whether we are male or female, Jewish or Croatian, or maybe Greeks (see Gal 3.26-39). When parents bring their newly born babies to be baptised, they carry out the act of 'presenting' them to God. We know that children are being baptised in the faith of their parents, which is the faith of the Church at the same time. The actual sacrament of baptism has the effect of annulling original sin and all other sins and receiving the Holy Spirit by which we become adopted children of God. But what kind of children we will be also depends on the actual presentation of the parents, which begins with baptism and continues throughout their life through their intercessory prayers.

The question is: 'What do parents actually want for their child in baptism?' The same question is asked by the priest who is baptising the child. Parents answer that they want baptism for their child, but often they do not know, nor do they wish to know, what that actually means. Wanting baptism means wanting to live the adopted life of a successor of Jesus Christ. It means that parents should wish for spiritual blessings for their child (to a close communion with God throughout their whole life) and secondly material blessings (health, blessing, honour, fertility...) although we should be aware that God can also give us all that, provided it does not represent a barrier to our spiritual growth. Material blessings for some can be a stimulant to be even closer to God, while for others they can become a reason to reject God because they feel they don't need Him, since they already have everything. Material blessings are only so when they lead to God! For it is better to be cursed in the eyes of others then spiritually dead!

Through baptism, parents have to accept Jesus' words which apply to everyone who follows him, i.e. who ever accepts Jesus Christ as their Savior and Redeemer. Those words don't promise blessings of this world, although they don't prevent them either, but they are second only to the real purpose of life; i.e. spiritual blessings. Jesus clearly tells us that the world will be against our kids if they decide to follow God and that most will have to pay a high price for their loyalty to God (see Lk 12.51-53; Lk 14.26-27; Lk 21.12-19; Mk 10.28-31; Mk 13.9-13; Mt 19.27-29). Are we as parents aware of that? Do we wish that for our children? If we truly love them, we will wish for it! If we do not wish for it, then we don't love them, probably not out of spite or selfishness, but rather out of ignorance. We need to spend more time reading passages of Sacred Scripture which speak about it! Reflecting on this we can form a correct inner attitude about what God expects from us through the sacrament of baptism, and how we should answer as parents who present our children to God through baptism and about accepting our own baptism with our own free will!

Let's further analyse the text about the presentation: Luke mentions two citizens of Israel who were just. When we read the Gospel we get the impression that the whole temple 'establishment' didn't want to accept Jesus as Messiah and that the Jewish temple was rife with corruption. But if we were to read carefully and reflect, we would see that the Gospel mentions other contemporaries of Jesus, temple officials who were good people of God, the priest Zechariah (father of John the Baptist), Nicodemus, Joseph from Arimathea, Simeon, and the prophetess Anna. So, God never leaves His people without saints; the Church of God was never left without saints. Sometimes the problem is we don't want to recognise or we cannot recognise them. God will always have enough saints in the Church - so hell will never overpower us.

God promised the old man Simeon that he wouldn't die until he had seen the newborn Messiah. Inspired by the Holy Spirit, he came to the temple when the Holy family were there; he took the child in his arms and said those words which amazed Mary and Joseph. But it wasn't the words themselves that gave them pleasure. Simeon didn't say anything that Mary didn't already know. He only cited the prophet Isaiah. In Israel then there wasn't anyone - if they took their faith seriously - who didn't know the book of Isaiah well. So Mary knew that the Messiah would be born of a virgin, that He would be a light that would illuminate the pagans and that he will be a glory to Israel. She knew that Jesus would be a downfall to many, and to others a reassurance, as well as a sign that would be disputed. But she also knew what Isaiah wrote about *the Suffering Servant*; she knew that Jesus would be killed. She knew it before the conception of Jesus was announced to her by the angel Gabriel. Already a deep love towards the Messiah who was to come, inhabited her mind and she already experienced the trauma of knowing that His death would be the death of a martyr. Mary had an awareness about the Messiah even before the angel announced it to her. She had already a clearly defined attitude towards Him in her heart.

The Jewish people persistently refused to believe the prophecy that talks about Jesus' suffering in Isaiah. Even the apostles refused to believe it. Mary though, had accepted this before His conception. The angel's annunciation and Mary's acceptance were the beginning of Mary's preparation for Jesus' sufferings. It is good to reflect that Mary accepted Jesus as the Messiah who was destined to suffer. What mother would willingly take a Son knowing that one day he would be brutally tortured and then killed? We can ask ourselves: Why did the Holy Spirit want Simeon to say those words so clearly in front of Mary and Joseph at the moment of the 'presentation', which should normally be a moment of rejoicing? The Evangelist wanted to tell us something clearly: That God wanted Mary and Joseph to present Jesus entirely so that they would visibly accept the future torture as God's will. And this is what they did. Mary from that moment onwards never even thought about trying to find ways to save her Son from the horrific fate that He was destined for, or to divert Him from it. Instead she reflected on how she would support Him to be able to withstand what awaited Him in those moments. Jesus knew what awaited Him and Mary gave Him strength throughout His life. So He knew that He was not going to be on His own in suffering: His Mother was going to support Him with her prayer and her 'correct attitude'. We will speak more about this in the sorrowful mysteries.

Let's ask ourselves if we would be able to accept it, if God in the future wanted one of our children to be tortured and killed in the prime of life because of his/her heroic witnessing to faith in Christ! Would we believe that God's 'offer' was a blessing for our child and for us as parents, or would we consider it a curse? The fact is, that this possibility is always there for those who want to present themselves completely for the salvation souls in life. Would we try to prevent our child from being a missionary or evangelizer, if we knew that he or she would surely be martyred or killed? Personally, I believe that that would be one of the greatest blessings my child could receive and that I, as a parent, could receive. I would gladly give God all my children to die a martyr's death testifying for Christ, but I would be even happier if it happened to me first so that they could follow my example! A few times now I have witnessed parents preventing their children from entering the seminary even though they really wanted to. Those parents believed it was a curse for their child to become a priest. That is so sad....

This mystery prepares us to be supportive towards our children in the proper way and when it is most needed, i.e. during the times of their worst trials. We mustn't think that we have to protect our children from all trials because it is impossible. Instead we have to be prepared to bring them to God through prayer and be with them in times of trial so that they can 'benefit' by gaining a closer relationship with God!

Parents who know the real truth should wish for imperishable values for their children, but they always have to pray for them too. The price will always be paid in *love for the world*. If we love this world more than the place where we will live in eternity, we will never be prepared to pay the price. The person who knows God will love heaven more than this world. Paul the apostle clearly writes: if we don't truly believe in the resurrection of the dead, then we should just eat and drink and enjoy ourselves in the way of the world because our faith is futile anyway. Paul doesn't mean that we have to believe in the mere existence of life after death, but rather, in what the Bible tells us about how life will be and with whom shall we live there.

Luke then mentions the prophetess Anna, the daughter of Phanuel. She was a woman who lived in the temple day and night, serving God by fasting and praying. Here we have a few very interesting facts. Through the Holy Spirit, she also recognized Jesus as the newly born Messiah and for that reason she began to glorify God. What is important to note, is that she began to talk about the newborn Messiah to everyone who was waiting for Him in Israel. Even before John the Baptist, the prophetess Anna was one of Jesus' first serious enunciators. She must have been well respected in the temple because of her holy way of life, but also because of the fact that she was a prophetess. She spent her whole life in the temple. We could almost say that she knew all the officials and regular visitors to the temple. Through these two people who were distinguished and recognized in Israel for their sanctity, the Holy Spirit announced the newborn Messiah and those that heard it could not forget or ignore that fact. If we put together the shepherds, the wise men from the east, Elizabeth, the old man Simeon and the prophetess Anna, we can see that for those who wanted to believe in the newborn Messiah, this satisfied them. When Jesus began His service of evangelizing, there were enough people in the temple who knew what had happened and in what way the Holy Spirit manifested Him as the foreseen Messiah. But even though there were people, acceptance of the Messiah was minimal.

How many people today who have heard numerous testimonies of God's existence and are aware of the power of Jesus' saving sacrifice, still don't want to accept Jesus as the Messiah and Saviour? They insist in believing that Jesus is only for 'holy people'. Holiness today is something which very few Christians wish for. Most people today *don't need* a Messiah. They didn't need him then! Few wanted Him as the Saviour of souls. Most wanted a Messiah who would renew their kingdom and bring prosperity and authority. That kind of a Messiah would be acceptable to most people, and to most Croatians too, a large percentage of which declare themselves to be Catholics! Unfortunately I have to admit that many *charismatics* desire the 'wrong' Messiah too.

Connection with the mystery

When we unite the mystery of Jesus' presentation with our lives and the lives of those for whom we are praying, we are reminded of baptism. We have to ask ourselves was our baptism united with the presentation of our lives in God's will? Was the attitude and prayer of our parents linked with the purpose of our baptism? If we were baptised as babies, we must present ourselves to the purpose of God's will as adults. We have to do everything with our personal will and spiritual efforts so the presentation becomes sincere. If we reflect a little deeper we will see that not many of us have really done that, and we come to understand how difficult it is to do. We will feel that *the superficial me* is fighting against that presentation and doesn't really want Jesus as the Messiah who brings new life. The depths at which a person can present themselves is something that usually takes time to develop. Few and far between are those who grow suddenly. Praying this mystery we await the grace to be able to present our lives to God so that we can accept His fatherhood and continue living the way His Son Jesus Christ lived. Through this mystery we will receive the grace to be able to present our children to God with the same feelings and expectations that Mary and Joseph had. This mystery also unites the baptism of other people who we are praying for with the mystery of Jesus' presentation and brings true light which opens the door to make the decision to sincerely present ones' life. The Holy Spirit will fill us even more and many can – praying this mystery – relive their birth.. In such a way we change our attitude towards our fellow-men, so our prayers for them are increasingly directed towards spiritual and less to materialistic needs.

Praying this mystery we can expect to receive through Mary's intercession:

- ♦ A presentation of our own personal life, this time accepting the power of baptism we received,

- ♦ A presentation of the lives of others, for whom we are praying, so that they can receive the grace of their baptism,

- ♦ A presentation of the lives of our children, who we given to be baptized with our own decision and in our faith,

- ♦ To be born again in the Holy Spirit by the presentation of our lives and accepting Jesus Christ as our Saviour and Redeemer, and a recognition of the Holy Spirit as God, who came to live in us and in whom we can and should live with our own spirit,

- ♦ Sincere repentance for not having completely presented ourselves or our children to God in baptism and the grace to pray for forgiveness from God, and for surrender,

- ♦ Our response to God's offer to become holy,

- ♦ The Holy Spirit opens our eyes so that we can see, ears so that we can hear and our hearts so that we can understand the plan He has for us and with people He puts on our path,

♦ Trust in God's love because we are presenting ourselves and others to Him,

♦ Everything else that the Holy Spirit puts in our heart as its grace during reading and reflection (meditation).

The fifth joyful mystery
– Mary finds Jesus in the Temple

Take a look at the Word of God!

(Lk 2.41-52)
"Now every year his parents went to Jerusalem for the festival of Passover. And when he was twelve years old, they went up as usual for the festival. When the festival was ended and they started to return, the boy Jesus stayed behind in Jerusalem, but his parents did not know it. Assuming that he was in the group of travellers, they went a day's journey. Then they started to look for him among their relatives and friends. When they did not find him, they returned to Jerusalem to search for him. After three days they found him in the temple, sitting among the teachers, listening to them and asking them questions. And all who heard him were amazed at his understanding and his answers. When his parents saw him, they were astonished; and his mother said to him, "Child, why have you treated us like this? Look your father and I have been searching for you in great anxiety." And he said to them, "Why were you searching for me? Did you not know that I must be in my Father's

*house?" But they did not understand what he
said to them. Then he went down with them
and came to Nazareth, and was obedient to
them. His mother treasured all these things in
her heart. And Jesus increased in wisdom and in
years and in divine and human favour."*

Let's analyse the text!

This mystery treats of the life of Jesus from the day
of his presentation in the temple up to the age of maturity - which in Jewish tradition - was twelve years of
age. The Bible tells us very little about it. We know that
He had to flee with His parents to Egypt and then after
Herod's death, they settled again in Nazareth. He was
with His parents. He had grown in wisdom, and God's
grace rested upon Him (see Lk 2:39-40). Luke tells us
that the Holy Family made a pilgrimage to Jerusalem
every year for the feast of the Passover. When Jesus
had turned twelve years of age, they went to make
their usual pilgrimage. In Israel back then at the age
of twelve, you were considered an adult after having
passed the exam in Mosaic Law. From then on, parents
weren't accountable for their children anymore.

They stayed in Jerusalem for a few days and soon
after the pilgrims, in larger or smaller convoys of wag-
ons, returned home. And so it was with the Holy Family. They left in the morning and travelled the whole
day. In the evening Mary and Joseph were concerned
because Jesus had not come to them. It was good to

take a rest. The convoy of people must have been large since Mary and Joseph hadn't noticed Jesus the whole time. When they realized He was not in the convoy, they returned to Jerusalem to find Him. It took them the whole day to walk to the city, but Saint Luke wrote that they barely managed to find Him the third day.

For three days Mary experienced 'to some extent' what she would go through in the three awful days following the death of her Son on the cross, when He would be lying in the tomb. It was not easy for her or for Joseph. In the Bible, it is the only incidence and probably the first time that we see something like 'disobedience'. Even though Jesus was filled with wisdom and the Holy Spirit, he had done something that – to a certain degree – was unadvisable: He stayed in Jerusalem without telling His parents.

They finally found Him in the Temple sitting amongst the teachers, listening and asking questions. Everyone present was admiring His wisdom. Mary and Joseph were astonished at the scene. They realized that Jesus – without having told them – deliberately stayed in the Temple. When they asked Him a question, they received a confusing answer or more specifically, a question in reply: "Why were you looking for me? Did you not know that I must be in my Father's house?" They did not understand what He said to them. Jesus returned with them to Nazareth and was obedient to them.

But what was on Mary's mind when her Son answered her in such way? Jesus was chosen to bring the

Good News to Israel. The Scriptures had clearly spoken about it. Only a small detail was missing. Namely, that Mary could not have known at what age Jesus would begin! Seeing her Son so mature and full of wisdom that He was teaching the teachers in the Temple, if they had accepted Him and admired Him so much - wouldn't Mary have asked herself had His time not already arrived? Everything seemed to point to it! Judging the whole incident (even though we haven't got a strong point of support) we could conclude that Jesus had most likely thought that, but Mary had thought differently. She knew His moment had not come and Jesus was obedient to her until He Himself realized that His moment had come. We can better understand it if we remember what happened at the wedding at Cana in Galilee.

Mary had showed outstanding wisdom and spiritual maturity confronting her Son like that, despite his being considered mature, wise and full of the Holy Spirit. It is a lesson that everyone should learn who wishes to follow the path of Jesus; especially those Christians who are called to important services inside the Church through various charismas. Often we believe that we must begin our mission or calling before God has ordained it, but only He knows the moment determined for us to 'begin'. Jesus had His Mother beside Him who - to a certain extent - 'prevented' Him from beginning too early. We too have a Mother who does the same thing for us, but only if we have enough trust in her.

That Mother is the Church! Take a look at the history of the Church and you will see how many times 'She' has acted prudently in similar situations. In order for that to happen to us, we have to be in obedience to the Church. In so far as we wish to put our trust in God, our obedience should be to the Church – the mystical body of which He is the head –then it becomes trust in God's providence. Saint Maximilian Kolbe defined obedience beautifully as trust in God's providence.

Sometimes we might feel like Jesus at the age of twelve if a Bishop or Parish Priest won't allow everything we want. But we don't have to be in despair about it.

If God has chosen us to serve Him in a certain way, He will find the best way, time and place for the beginning of our work. Maybe the time hasn't arrived because we, or those who we have to serve, are not yet fully ready. It is also possible that a Parish Priest or Bishop might make a wrong judgement or make a mistake - but we would make an even bigger mistake by not listening to them. If God lights your lamp, He will put it on the table – and not under the table – to illuminate and no force will be able to prevent it. God does everything with a reason, even though He mightn't give the Parish Priest or the Bishop the ability to judge the situation well (by our criteria!); it still doesn't mean that He made a mistake. Maybe He wants to test our obedience to show us what we are like?

Connection with the mystery

Uniting our life with Jesus' through this joyful mystery we are preparing ourselves for similar situations in life. Through this mystery Mary is teaching us obedience to the Holy Spirit. We have to realize that for so many events in our life we need spiritual maturity, which requires not only wisdom and knowledge, but also life experience - which no school can give. Every Christian testifies by the way they live their life, and his/her service too has to be testified to by our lives. Before we rush 'too early' to achieve something, try to 'see' everything that happens in our life through God's eyes, so that it can become an invaluable pearl of experience. Experience consists in perseverance and endurance in adversity. The two virtues are so necessary for humbly and successfully administering every service in the Kingdom of God and they can be arrived at only through personal life experience.

I have already said that this mystery takes in everything which has happened in our soul from birth to full maturity. At the same time the most important were the first few months after conception and the first year. A lot of families experience various negativities which leave a deep mark on the soul. Our attitude towards God, ourselves, people closer to us and the world in general has to be healed so that it will not influence negatively. I will mention a few possible negative situations in which we might have been found as children:

- One or both parents might not have been present due to death, divorce or any other sort of separated life,
- Lack of acceptance by one parent,
- Alcoholism in the family,
- Severe and frequent arguments between parents,
- Poverty in the negative sense,
- Parents lack of faith,
- One parent being seriously ill,
- Illness in childhood, painful treatment of the illness, and/or separation from parents due to treatment,
- Degradation and rejection in the environment,
- Loneliness, growing up without brothers, sisters and friends,
- Parents inability to dedicate more attention to their child due to work,
- Parents disappointment with our appearance and gender,
- Abuse from a parents or guardian,
- The feeling of abandonment by a close person,
- A denial of attention, gentleness or acknowledgement
- Nightmares and various sorts of fear,

♦ Many other influences which you can come across or read about in books which deal with inner healing.

I will give three examples so that you can understand the influence of an *unhealed wound of the soul* on our lives.

First example

Mark was born as a twin. His birth was a big surprise for everyone in the large family. He was born very small so they had given him a name straight away and took him to church so he wouldn't die unbaptised. His twin brother was different in so far as he was a normally developed baby. His parents had not held out too much hope in Marks life, but it seems that baptism had made a difference: God decided to spare him. After a certain time he caught up physically, and even overtook his twin brother and everything finished well. When he grew up and got married, his wife had certain problems. At least that's what he thought! Namely, she became irritated when he began to act differently in the company of young girls, i.e. how he wanted to appeal to them in a not so 'unobtrusive' way. After a number of warnings, Mark agreed to 'examine his behaviour'. At the next encounter with young girls, he had to admit that his whole being was beginning to act a little 'disorderly'. There were no impure thoughts, just a wish to be accepted, an exaggerated attempt to attract attention to himself. He had to acknowledge that he was doing something he couldn't control. When he admitted to himself that a problem existed which had to be solved, he began to pray to the Holy Spirit to show him the roots of the problem and to heal them. After a short period of time the Holy Spirit gave him a vision showing the cause of his behaviour and with that, liberated him of the problem. So what was it about? Mark's mother had more children, so she was very busy she couldn't take care of the newborn twins on her own. So she handed that responsibility over to his two older sisters. In a vision, Mark saw his Mother asking his two older sisters to choose which of the twins they would take care of. At that moment, not one of them wanted Mark. Both were scared of bonding with a brother who might 'die in the near future'. The rejection was hysterical, typical of the behaviour of children so the mother had to impose a choice. The sister, who received Marko to take care of, quickly grew to love him and everything was forgotten. Reliving the situation in the vision Marko felt the abandonment very intensely which made him cry. The crying brought him healing and liberation. Later he asked his Mother about it and she actually confirmed everything.

Second example

Ivan was a very good and religious child and he really wanted St. Nicholas to bring him a soccer ball. He liked playing soccer but he didn't have a ball. For a whole month he regularly went to Mass, regularly prayed, he listened to his parents and he even did jobs which no one asked him to do. He felt sure that God would reward him for his efforts and send a ball with St. Nicholas. The year before he didn't get what he wanted so he came to the conclusion he didn't make a big enough effort. So in that year he gave everything of himself so that the soccer ball would not 'escape' him. Morning came and he had to take a look at the gifts. There was no end to Ivan's disappointment: there was no ball. He was even more disappointed when he found out his neighbour received the ball he had wished for. For a second, he thought St. Nicholas made a mistake with the address, but it was not logical. His disappointment was even greater because his friend never made an effort for a ball, but he had received one. He didn't learn or help his parents. His family never went to Mass regularly. He didn't pray to God. But still he was the one to receive the ball! Now Ivan came to the conclusion that God's understanding of 'fairness' is very different to his. As if it didn't pay to be good. He decided not to allow God to disappoint him again. He made a firm decision that he would continue to pray, and to be a good and obedient child, that he would go to Mass and the other sacraments regularly, but there is one thing he would never ever do again: he would never ever again in his life expect anything from God; he would find his own way. He would continue being religious so that he wouldn't end up in hell but he wouldn't expect anything from God. On one occasion he heard a charismatic say that God wants and will do everything for a person and when he heard that it caused uncontrollable fury in him. I often see the same fury in people at seminars and spiritual retreats when they see that God is healing people. But what happened with Ivan? Two days spent in Medjugorje was enough to completely change his attitude and to once again expect a lot from God. In Medjugorje, he didn't experience anything unusual with humanly speaking. But seeing people who had put their trust in God, their deep joy and peace helped him to receive inner healing from the feeling of abandonment by God!

Third example

I had been in the service of evangelization already for many years and my housing problem wasn't solved. Even though I was earning relatively well, I was never able to earn enough to solve my housing problem. Money would always 'slide' through my fingers. Something always tore, broke and there were always unforeseen expenses which wouldn't allow me save enough money. I prayed for thousands of people by then and many of them through prayer of faith experienced a response to God's love. I prayed to God for my problem. But he had done nothing to change it. I began to help him in that. I suggested he send me rich people, who are in need and who I will pray for. After the prayers they would probably see I haven't solved my housing problem and maybe ask me if I need anything. God had heard my prayers, but only – half of them! Namely, rich people had come; I prayed for them, they received grace, but not one of them thought of asking me if I needed anything. The situation became critical. The second baby was on the way and our rented apartment was too small for one baby let alone two. I have very little time but I decided to pray even harder. That 'harder' meant that I was practically yelling to God to help me. I will never forget how God due to the tremendous yelling decided to answer me. I clearly heard his voice: "I want to but I can't!" I was very surprised! I tried to convince him that He was Almighty, He was God and everything that existed on this planet belonged to Him and He could do anything He wanted. But the convincing wasn't successful. Then I did the most intelligent thing: I asked him, "Why can't you?"

Very shortly I had a vision that showed me what happened. There were eight of us children and one year there was four of us going to school. It wasn't always easy purchasing that many books, accessories, clothes and shoes. Even though my parents were both diligent and thrifty (I carried the same bag for four years and shoes I would get one pair a year) that year instead of receiving tennis shoes I received a kind of shoes that looked like tennis shoes. Even today after thirty years I can still remember them – as if I had them only yesterday. I and my twin brother were the best students at school so my parents thought that the 'alternative shoes' would pass. But they didn't pass. After I had been humiliated because of my shoes, a teacher sent me home for tennis shoes. I knew I didn't have tennis shoes at home. In a vision I saw that scene when the teacher sent me home. I saw myself standing on the opposite side of the school and I was saying something. I heard the words clearly. I wanted to avoid further disappointment due to poverty (the tennis shoes were just the tip of the iceberg), so I decided to create a defence mechanism. These sorts of mechanisms children often create and then later in life they have big problems. My defence mechanism was a firm inner decision-oath, which sounded something like this: "I never want to be rich! I don't like rich people! They're selfish. They only think about themselves! I don't want to have anything in life! I will be intelligent and happy!" I it engraved on stone in my soul that I didn't want financial blessings. When I saw the vision I repented, I prayed for forgiveness and I said to God that I want to have enough of everything and some extra so I can help others (see 2 Cor 9.8-9). After that prayer I began building a house and people were coming to help. They offered me money without credit for the amount of years I needed. Within a year and a half, I moved into my own new house after years of being a tenant. I also bought a better car soon afterwards, but there is no end to this story. The Catholic Charismatic Renewal based in the Vatican suggested that I be the one to take care of raising funds for their needs. Is not our God a mighty God?!

Therefore, uniting with the fifth joyful mystery we can expect to receive Mary's mediation in:

♦ Inner healing of wounds received in childhood and further on in life,

♦ The strength to forgive everyone who has hurt us in any way,

♦ Liberation from harmful and misguided vows, which have become defence mechanisms to stave off further disappointments,

♦ The help of the Holy Spirit in spiritual development,

♦ Wisdom for life,

♦ Everything that the Holy Spirit reveals to us through Mary's advocacy.

Conclusion

Praying the rosary unites our life with Jesus' life. We go through our own life immersing ourselves in the mysteries of Jesus' life together with Mary. Through her mediation we give our own life to God, part by part. At the same time through the enlightening of the Holy Spirit we see ourselves the way we are: weak and sinful, in need of God's love. The weaker we are the more humble we become and therefore dependent on God. Acknowledging the truth about God and ourselves we start to see our neighbour in a different light. Slowly but surely our judgement turns to pity, and then into love.

Through unification in prayer we experience healing and liberation. Our life receives its purpose. We get a taste of the character and personality of God's children and in that way we become more capable of 'understanding' God's offer to accept His Fatherhood.

We become more aware of God's constant presence, and how He turns everything into good for those who love and believe in Him. In our life we won't be liberated and healed of everything that is bothering us. We won't always be able to understand the purpose of a lot of things happening in our lives. Nevertheless, praying the rosary ensures us that we will receive faith in God and trust in His Word, hope and eternal life and love towards God, ourselves and those around us. And all of that to a degree we can carry.

The rosary is a prayer of faith, hope and love. If everything else disappears, those three always remain!

Table of contents

Translators note: Having consulted Scriptural Theologians, the author was advised that (with regard to the theme of this book), the NRSV Bible is the most exact translation of the original. For this reason all biblical quotations in the English translation of *Bakina Krunica* have been taken from the NRSV Catholic Edition / Oxford University Press.